D0606862

The *Water Garden* DESIGN BOOK

The Water Garden DESIGN BOOK

YVONNE REES
and
PETER MAY

BARRON'S

A QUARTO BOOK

ISBN 0-7641-5373-0

Library of Congress Catalog Card No. 00-110919

QUAR.TWGD
Conceived, designed, and produced by
Quarto Publishing plc
The Old Brewery
6 Blundell Street
London N7 9BH

Senior Project Editor Nicolette Linton
Senior Art Editor Sally Bond
Assistant Art Director Penny Cobb
Text Editors Peter Kirkham, Pat Farrington
Designer Paul Wood
Illustrators Kuo Kang Chen, Ann Savage
Picture Research Laurent Boubounelle
Indexer Pamela Ellis

Art Director Moira Clinch
Publisher Piers Spence

Manufactured by Regent Publishing Services Ltd, Hong Kong
Printed by Leefung-Asco Printers Ltd, China

9 8 7 6 5 4 3 2 1

contents

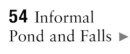

◀ Bring the drama of the wild to your back door with a large rockery waterfall.

introduction

Rabbit-ear iris

Water is the most exciting element you can use in garden design. It can offer new perspectives, a note of drama, movement, light, sound, and constantly changing reflections. It is flexible enough to adapt to any size or shape of garden, and even the smallest water feature makes an instant focal point. Yet once installed, whether a large pond or a modest patio fountain, it becomes one of the easiest areas of the garden to maintain, the ideal concept for today's busy lifestyles and modern garden philosophy, which demands maximum impact for minimum effort.

No wonder then that water is an essential tool in the repertoire of every modern garden designer and landscaper. Forget large expanses of grass and labor-intensive borders. Large ponds edged with colored decking are frequently used to transform the smallest backyard; a dingy corner becomes a symphony of bubbling water and exotic foliage plants; or a large plot is divided into new, more interesting areas by canals and water courses crossed by bridges and stepping stones.

▶ The excitement of a water cascade and a tranquil pool ringed by lush plants have transformed this sloping garden.

▲ A good planting scheme quickly disguises water feature construction with a totally natural result.

Water is perfect for disguising the true size and shape of a plot. With the addition of an electric pump, the possibilities are extended further: into decorative ideas, such as fountains, water spouts, and sculptures—and dramatic features such as waterfalls, streams, and cascades. Your garden is given an instant focus: the sound of trickling or cascading water is a wonderful lure, even before it is visible. A bubbling barrel or freestanding formal fountain will stand quite happily on any backyard patio, balcony or roof garden, with the added advantage that it can be taken with you when you move. A large rocky waterfall or stainless steel cascade will effectively set the scene in a larger garden, adding height and drama to your scheme. Don't forget front gardens too: a little sparkle and splash makes a stylish welcome and takes up hardly any space.

It is not just the design and decorative benefits that make water such a worthwhile addition to the garden. A pond or stream offers the chance to grow a wider range of delightful plants: those that prefer damp conditions, or that will grow in or on the water's surface. Bog plants—species that enjoy moist, waterlogged soil—tend to have exotic or large, architectural foliage that make a dramatic addition to the garden. Marginal plants include some of the most beautiful flowering and foliage forms such as iris, arum lilies, and rushes; and the smallest expanse of water can be used to display that most beautiful of blooms, the water lily.

A pond, a pool, or a patio barrel also provides the opportunity to keep fish; you can have hours of pleasure observing their lazy antics, or enjoy their tameness as they swim to the side to be fed, and they will add color and movement to your water feature. Extend your fishkeeping to the handsome koi, and you may even find yourself with a new, absorbing hobby. There will be other pond life to observe as well: the smallest pond acts as a magnet to wildlife, and surprisingly quickly your garden will become home to a wider range of birds, not to mention frogs, newts, and spectacular-looking dragonflies, and with absolutely no effort on your part.

Then there are the therapeutic effects: a garden is somewhere to relax, your personal slice of paradise, and what better place to unwind after a hard day at work than beside the shimmer of water, watching the reflection of clouds passing by and listening to the soothing splash or spatter of water. You can enhance the effect with an oriental theme to your water feature; or by adding specially designed sculptural cascades and fountains designed to improve your environment.

So how can you enjoy all these benefits and achieve the stunning visual effects of the professional garden designers in your own backyard? Time spent planning and choosing the right features is essential to success. It always pays to think big, even when designing for small areas, so don't skimp on size, as water features are hard to change once installed. Style is important

Purple loosestrife

too, as it will influence the rest of your garden scheme. Do you want a strictly formal look? Or is a more rustic theme your dream? A water feature combined with the right plants and accessories can capture a Mediterranean feel, oriental serenity, or all the drama of the jungle. It helps to have a clear idea of what you are aiming for. There are practical points to consider too before you start building, such as proximity to trees and other features, access for maintenance, a convenient supply of electricity, light and shade, height of your water table, and drainage.

Careful construction is also essential to success: always check the technical details of your chosen feature, especially if they involve a skill new to you, and employ a qualified electrican where necessary. Water features are unlike any other area of the garden; you will have to be not just a landscaper, but also builder, technician, and possibly fishkeeper. Safety is paramount especially if you have young children. Take all precautions and get the details right, and you will be rewarded by an exciting, relaxing, and easy-to-care-for water garden.

Water lily

Hosta fortunei 'Aurea Marginata'

▼ Give a traditional pond a contemporary feel with sculptural 'sails', timber decking, and a curvaceous, staggered bridge.

▲ Before you can create a fabulous water feature like this Japanese-style pond, you will need to familiarize yourself with the basics of water garden design.

The Essentials

You may already have some idea of the water feature you wish to create, possibly inspired by a pond seen in a magazine, on a show, or on a television program. Where should you begin?

before you *start*

Careful planning and preparation, and the right equipment and techniques for the job are key to a successful result. Size and position will be your first consideration, and there are a number of elements to bear in mind when creating your own water feature.

A pond needs an open sunny site with some shade if the water is not to turn green, but keep it away from deciduous trees to avoid leaf fall. Don't excavate close to your garden boundaries, and take note of the position of any drains and cables. Also consider linking existing features and the pond for a natural look. As soon as you have chosen the style, size, and position of your feature, mark out the course with sand, a length of hose, or wooden pegs and string.

▲ Even the smallest water feature can be designed with plenty of interest.

LEVELING THE SITE

Mark out a level site, especially where the ground is uneven.

❶ Put in your first wooden peg to mark the proposed water level. This will be your marker or datum peg.

❷ Use a straightedge (a length of planed, warp-free wood or piece of metal) and a level to align your other marker pegs with it.

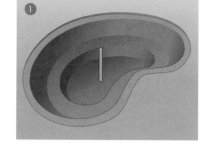

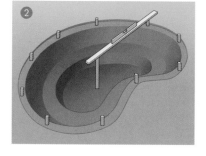

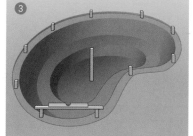

❸ Check your planes across the excavation and around the perimeter with a level. Dig out and fill to correct any unevenness in the site.

SHAPING A POOL

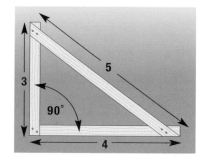

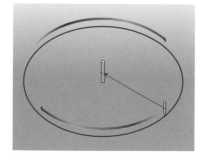

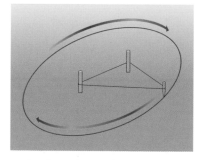

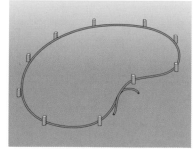

To create an accurate right-angle for a formal square or rectangle, make yourself a scaled-up set square using lengths of timber in the ratio 3:4:5 to guarantee a 90° angle.

To draw a circular shape, use a center stake 4 feet x 2 inches x 2 inches (1.2 m x 5 cm x 5 cm) and a length of string to define a circle, marked with pegs or sand.

Draw an oval with two fixed stakes and a loop of string. Place the loop over the stakes and, using a sharp stick to keep the string taut, mark out an elliptical shape on the ground.

An irregular, informal shape can be mapped out using sand, a garden hose, or wooden pegs 1 foot x 1 inch x 1 inch (30 cm x 2.5 cm x 2.5 cm), and string.

EXCAVATION

Only the smallest ponds can be dug out by hand using a pick and shovel. Wherever possible, it is better to rent a mechanical digger and finish off with the hand tools. Tool rental may seem expensive, but machinery can be rented at a special rate over a weekend and is well worth it in the time and effort it will save you.

DIGGING YOUR POND

① Remove the turf to a depth of 2 inches (5 cm). Roll up into strips, soil side out, and keep them damp until ready to reuse in the garden.

② Dig out to a depth of 9 inches (23 cm). Mark out a deep zone of 12 inches (30 cm) if creating a marginal shelf. Dig out the rest of the area to the required depth. If you are planning to keep fish, a depth of 24 inches (60 cm) is necessary; for koi it is more like 5 feet (1.5 m).

③ If digging out mechanically, finish shaping and leveling by hand, using a spade. Check the level of the pond around the perimeter, using a straightedge and level.

④ Once dug, rake over the bottom of pool to remove any stones, roots, or sharp objects. Spread a 1-inch (2.5-cm) deep layer of sand over the base as a further protection for the liner.

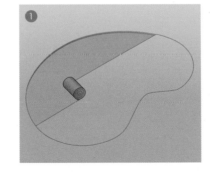

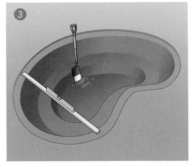

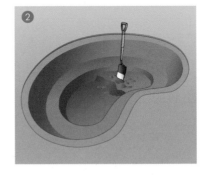

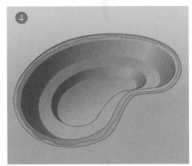

MECHANICAL DIGGERS

Various machines are available for rent, depending on the size of hole you wish to dig and whether you need to move large quantities of soil. Most diggers can be hired on a daily or weekly basis, with special rates for a weekend. Bigger machines with a professional operator are hired by the hour, but may work out to be less expensive since you do not have to spend time getting used to using the machine yourself. More importantly, you will have to consider how you are going to get the machine into your garden; if necessary, diggers can be winched over a garden fence. You will also need to consider how you are going to dispose of the excavated soil, so you may also have to rent something to haul it away.

HAND TOOLS

Make sure you have all the tools you require for the job before you start. You'll find most of them already in your tool shed. A pickax is useful for breaking up hard soils. You will also need a spade or garden fork and a shovel. Don't forget some means of transporting the excavated soil; a sturdy wheelbarrow with an inflatable tire is best for heavy loads. You will also need a small fork and a trowel for planting.

► You may already have most of the hand tools required.

◄ A mechanical digger will be necessary for all but the smallest pools.

LINE YOUR POND

Whether you choose a rigid or flexible liner, it is essential to make the necessary preparations before it is laid or your efforts will be wasted. Double check that your excavations are level and go over the whole area to make sure there are no sharp objects.

CHOOSING A LINER

You can buy a ready-made liner prefabricated in rigid fiberglass, which is suitable for raised or sunken pools. There is a wide range of both formal and informal styles available, some of which include a marginal shelf and even an integral filter. You can also buy preformed shapes for streams and waterfalls. To install, simply excavate a hole to the same size and shape but slightly larger than the rigid liner, line with sand and hardcore, and lower the liner into position. Gradually fill the pool with water, backfilling with soil as you go and checking frequently that the top is level using a straightedge and level.

The alternative is a flexible PVC or longer-lasting and more expensive butyl liner. Flexible liners are available in packs or cut to length from a roll. Calculate as closely as possible how much you need, as wastage is expensive. The liner will stretch to allow for ledges and will be pushed into contours by the weight of the water.

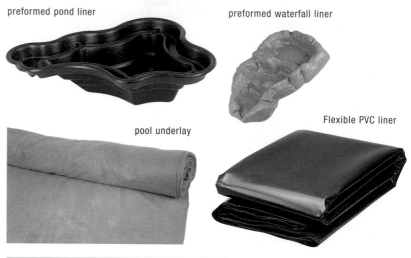

preformed pond liner

preformed waterfall liner

pool underlay

Flexible PVC liner

▲ Pond liners come in many shapes and sizes.

CALCULATING POND LINER

- Sheet length = pond length + 2 x pond depth + 24 inches (60 cm)

- Sheet width = pond width + 2 x pond depth + 24 inches (60 cm)

LAYING FLEXIBLE LINER

Once the excavation is prepared with a layer of sand, you will need to line it with pool underlay or old carpet to cushion the liner. It will be easier to lay the liner on a warm day, so that it remains as flexible as possible. Open the packet and leave overnight in a warm room if necessary.

❶ Lay the lining material over the excavated hole, making sure that there is an even amount of excess all the way around. Loosely tuck and fold it into place. Weigh it down with round stones or bricks around the perimeter.

❷ Start filling the pool slowly with water using a hose. As the pool fills, the weight of the water will push the liner into place. Keep adjusting the liner, folding and tucking if necessary to get the smoothest possible fit.

❸ When the pond is filled to the required level, cut away any excess liner, leaving around 12 inches (30 cm) to be tucked into the soil and disguised by your chosen pond edging.

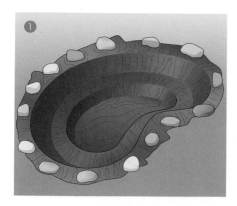

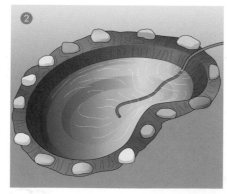

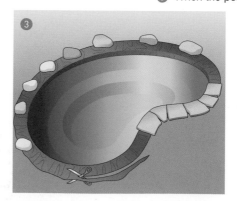

LINING WITH CONCRETE

Concrete makes a strong lining that is suitable for formal ponds and watercourses, providing it is properly mixed and applied. Small areas can be mixed by hand, but for larger areas, rent a mechanical mixer or order a delivery of ready-mixed concrete. If using ready-mixed, make sure the site is absolutely ready before the concrete arrives. Level, shape, and excavate the pond, then cover the surface area in 0.75 inch (19 mm) chicken wire.

1 Mix the concrete to the required dimensions (6:1 sand:cement). Use a bucket to calculate the ingredients and mix them in a mechanical mixer or on a large plywood board (never on your pavement or tarmac) until they are evenly distributed. Add water until the mixture is stiff, like porridge. Add colorings, antifrost or water-proofing solutions at this stage.

2 Apply the mixture to the sides and base of your pond or pool, using a concreting trowel, to a thickness of around 6 inches (15 cm), working it well into the chicken wire. The mixture should be stiff enough not to slump to the base of the pond.

3 Angling the sides at about 20° from the perpendicular should make shuttering unnecessary, but the sides can be shuttered using wood to keep the concrete in place until it has dried. Nail pieces of timber around the inside of the excavation allowing sufficient space for the chicken wire and concrete layer. Remove the wood when the concrete is dry.

4 When you reach the top edge of the pond, recess the concrete into the bank with a 3-inch (7.5-cm) notch, removing the leveling peg before the concrete dries.

5 Finish the sides and base of the pond with a float to produce a smooth finish. Leave to dry.

How much concrete do I need?

To calculate the amount of concrete you need for a pool, add the surface area of the sides to that of the base and multiply by the thickness of the concrete, usually around 6 inches (15 cm). It is better to overestimate than underestimate, as the feature will have to be constructed in one go.

CONCRETE TIPS

● Measure materials accurately; never rely on guesswork.

● Keep all the ingredients clean and free from soil or other debris.

● If the cement powder is damp or lumpy and refuses to crumble between the fingers, don't use it.

● Mix concrete with clean water, but never add extra water to the mix, as this will affect its strength.

● Only concrete when the weather is dry but not hot, with no risk of frost.

● Keep a sheet or tarpaulin nearby to cover your work should the weather change for the worse.

● Flush out the the toxic lime from a concrete pond with three changes of water and wait for three months before stocking with fish and plants.

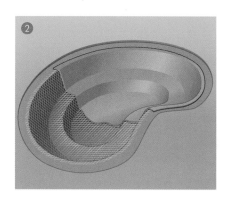

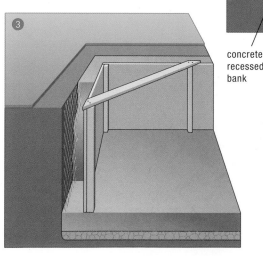

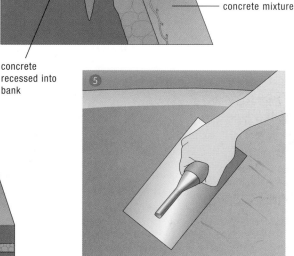

compacted rubble

leveling peg

chicken wire

concrete mixture

concrete recessed into bank

LIGHT, AIR, AND MOVEMENT

A garden pond or stream cannot sustain the ideal ecological conditions of a natural feature, so if you want to run some kind of moving water feature, keep fish, and maintain your water crystal clear, you will require a little mechanical assistance. Although solar-powered pumps are available, this generally means you need an electrical supply in the garden.

PUMPS

Pumps come in a range of sizes and can be used to run a fountain, filter, waterfall, or a combination of these, if powerful enough, using a T-piece in the outlet pipe. Low-voltage submersible pumps (sumps) that remain beneath the water are easier to install and maintain than above-ground models, which can be more powerful but require weatherproof housing and safe connection to the mains. It is better to overestimate the size of pump; your supplier can advise you depending on the size of feature you wish to power. Pump specifications are usually measured as flow rate per hour and maximum head of water. They are calculated on the widest bore of tubing for maximum performance; the length of pipe and the number of bends will also affect performance. "Head" relates to the height the water can be pumped in relation to the water level in the pond.

▲ You will need to choose the right size pump for your convenience.

SAFETY FIRST

● All exterior cables, connections, and fittings to the mains should be installed by a qualified electrician.

● Always install a circuit breaker (RCD) that will cut off the supply immediately there is a short circuit.

● Cables must be protected by a conduit, to avoid accidental damage by digging in the garden.

● All connections must be waterproof and approved for outdoor use.

● Low-voltage pumps are available for smaller features and can be a safer option.

Weatherproof cable connectors

SETTING UP A PUMP

❶ If you are using the pump with a built-in filter, push it onto the inlet pipe until it clicks into place.

❷ If you are intending to power more than one feature, push a T-piece adaptor onto the outlet pipe of the pump. Alternatively, screw on a blanking cap.

❸ Fit an adjusting screw so that you can control the flow of water.

❹ Lower the pump gently into the pond, raising it on to a plinth or brick if necessary. Connect it to your chosen feature and plug it into a suitable electrical supply.

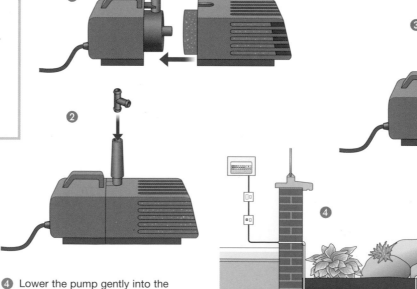

FILTERS

A filter system will keep your water clean and healthy, and is especially important if you keep fish, as the ammonia and nitrite compounds in fish waste must be removed to keep them healthy.

Filter systems are based mainly on a mechanical prefilter to remove larger debris; a biological filter, which converts toxic waste into plant-nutritious nitrate; and an ultraviolet clarifier, which eliminates the pea soup effect of overactive algae. The mechanical filter removes larger debris with brushes and sponges; it is more efficient if fitted with a vortex prestrainer. The water is pumped through the biological filter, which employs a bacterial colony that lives in special material in the filter chambers. It takes four to six weeks for the colony to become fully active, although this process can be speeded up using a proprietary starter solution. You must keep the filter running non-stop or the colony will die. If you have fish, consider using a back-up pump in case of failure. An ultraviolet clarifier is useful for keeping the water clear, but the bulb does need checking about once a month, and replacing annually.

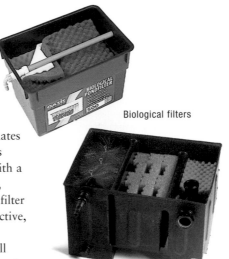

Biological filters

Ultraviolet clarifier

LIGHTING

With low-voltage fixtures reducing the risk of accidents associated with outdoor electricity, water and lighting are a marriage made in heaven. Not only does garden lighting extend use of your patio or garden after dark, but underwater lighting, and spotlights can also look spectacular.

You can combine the power supply to your lights with other water garden features such as pumps and filters, but you must take into account the total power load per cable. The length the cable has to run will make a difference: voltage levels will drop over longer distances; you may have to plan for a thicker cable or several cables for the power load. Exterior cables must be protected by a conduit and buried to a depth of at least 18 inches (45 cm) to avoid disturbance when digging. Or run the cable along a wall or fence; clip it safely out of reach with special fixing clips. If an exterior electricity supply is not practical, investigate solar-powered lighting.

When choosing electrical fixtures, remember that operating them separately gives greater flexibility. Some are designed to be seen; but, as a general rule, they should be concealed in the ground or hidden under foliage, in trees or among wall climbers.

◄ ▲ Underwater spotlights may be purchased singly or in sets of two or three.

AERATORS AND BUBBLERS

Fish need oxygen to keep healthy and at certain times of year, this can be in short supply in the water. If on hot, thundery, summer days you see your fish gasping on the surface of the pond, you know the oxygen levels have dropped dangerously low, and your fish are at risk. A moving water feature such as a cascade or fountain can help replenish oxygen supplies; but if you are keeping koi, or your pond is quite heavily stocked, consider using an electrical aerator or bubbler during hotter weather.

► An aerator may be necessary in summer for well-stocked fish pools.

SAFETY FIRST

● Use only lighting recommended for outdoor use and choose a good quality make. Avoid badly fitting components and inferior materials.

● Unless you have experience of installing electricity outdoors, enlist the help of a qualified contractor to install your pond and garden system.

● All exterior wiring should be fitted with a residual current-operated circuit breaker which cuts the power off automatically at the slightest deviation in the current.

CHOOSE YOUR WATER FEATURE

Even the smallest water feature will add a magical new element to your garden design. Take care to position your chosen feature where it will make the most impact and add a moving water device like a fountain or waterfall for extra sparkle and interest.

RAISED PONDS

A raised pond brings fish and plants to eye-level and, with a wide coping or integral seating, is the perfect place to sit and observe your pond at close quarters. Raised features are also ideally suited to wheelchair water gardeners, who can maintain and enjoy their pond without assistance. Raised ponds look particularly good as part of a patio complex, where edgings can be matched to other hard landscaping materials nearby, or the pool linked to raised beds, seating, or even a barbecue. A particularly stylish option where a change of level is desired is a series of raised ponds on different levels linked by a simple cascade.

▶ This large raised pond at the end of a pathway creates a marvelous focal point.

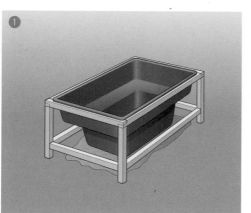

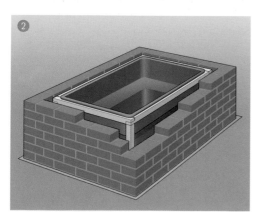

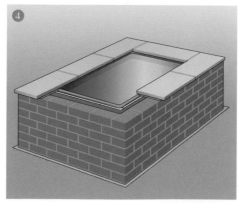

INSTALLING A RAISED POND

One of the easiest ways to install a raised pond is to use a fiberglass, preformed liner. The liner needs to be placed on a concrete slab, cushioned with a 4 inch (10 cm) layer of sand, then boxed in and backfilled to keep it stable.

❶ Position the liner on the sand and build a simple wooden frame around to keep it in place.

❷ Construct a suitable facing around the pond: concrete blocks with a render finish, bricks, paving, or timbers would all be suitable. Bring the edging up level with the top of the pond.

❸ Start filling the pond slowly, using a hose, backfilling between the liner and the facing with soil as it fills up.

❹ When the pond is full, overlap the edging at the rim, using flat slabs or coping stones, or a wooden rim if faced with timbers, in order to hide the liner and make a neat finish. If wide enough, the sill could double as a seat.

FOUNTAINS

Fountains make a great focal point and come in a wide choice of sizes and styles for all locations. Once you have installed a pump, all you need is a fountain nozzle, a length of plastic tubing, and jubilee clips to connect them. Nozzles and jets offer different spray patterns, from tall plumes to low bell-like effects for smaller ponds. Some fountain kits even come complete with underwater lighting. If you want something more ornamental, the fixture can be attached to a spouting figure or a modern sculpture. It is important that the spray is not higher than half the diameter of the pond, or you will lose water over the sides.

You don't even need a pond to enjoy a fountain feature: elegant freestanding units are available; alternatively, arrange the spout to emerge from a wall-mounted head, creature, or even a simple tap, into a bowl or concealed reservoir. Another child-safe fountain idea is the bubble fountain, which operates from a hidden sump dug into the ground. The water bubbles out over a millstone or pile of boulders placed on a grid over the sump.

◄ A series of rocky falls makes a dramatic feature for larger, informal gardens.

▲ A bell fountain looks best in small pools.

Hose

'T' hose connector

Hose clips

► The tall plume style fountain makes plenty of splash.

WATERFALLS AND CASCADES

A waterfall makes a lovely feature in conjunction with a pond, adding height and movement to the garden and providing the opportunity to plan a rocky area with interesting alpine plants. It can also be a useful way to utilize the spoil from excavating a pond. Importantly, you need a pump powerful enough to cope with the volume of water, especially if you are running a fountain or filter from the same pump via a T-piece connector. It is worth taking the time and trouble to get it looking right before the water is turned on: take care to arrange the rocks and boulders to look as natural as possible and fill the pockets between them with soil for softening plants. Alternatively, a modern cascade might send sheets of water down a wall of brick or Perspex.

▲ Semi-formal stream with pebbles and a decked bridge.

STREAMS AND RILLS

A stream, or that more formal watercourse, a rill, is a superb feature for dividing the garden into more interesting areas, and for incorporating bridges and stepping stones. Generally, it should be built in the same way as a pond, by excavating and lining, checking your levels at every stage. The stream or rill should be completely level, or the water will simply run to the bottom of the feature and wait to be pumped to the top again. If installing on a sloping site, you will have to create a series of small holding pools, linked by weirs, to achieve a satisfactory effect. For an informal look, run the water over stones and boulders between the pools. A more formal rill might pass from one level to the next by means of perforated bricks or a Perspex lip.

▲ Different sizes of boulders and pebbles add atmosphere at the water's edge.

MAKING A PEBBLE BEACH

A pebble beach makes a delightful edging to an informal pond and is essential for wildlife pools, where it allows birds, reptiles, and small mammals safe access to the water's edge. You will need to create a gently sloping bank on one side when excavating your pond.

❶ When calculating how much liner you require, allow sufficient extra material to run up the gently sloping bank. Secure the liner under the turf bank, a bog area, or paving as appropriate.

❷ Lay irregular but rounded pebbles over the liner to create the beach. Run the pebbles right down into the water for the best effect.

CREATING A BOG GARDEN

A bog garden with its large and beautiful sculptural plants makes a wonderful companion to an informal pond, or an alternative feature where a sunken pond might not be practical. If space is really limited, you can create a mini bog garden by sinking one or more barrels in the ground and filling with moist soil and a couple of moisture-loving plants. Cover the immediate area with pebbles to soften the effect and maintain a damp environment.

❶ Remove turf from the site and excavate the desired area to a depth of around 14 inches (35 cm).

❷ Cover with a large sheet of PVC or butyl lining material, held in place with large, smooth boulders that will not damage the material.

❸ Use a garden fork to puncture the bottom of the liner with drainage holes—about one hole per square yard/meter. Add a layer of 0.75 inch clean chippings, 4 to 6 inches deep. Place turf upside down on top.

❹ Top with a good moisture-retaining compost and soak thoroughly before planting.

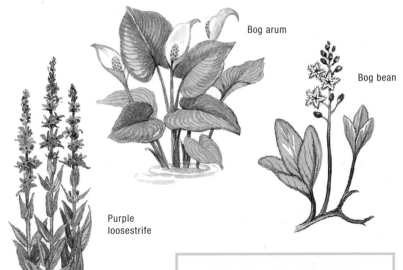

Bog arum

Bog bean

Purple loosestrife

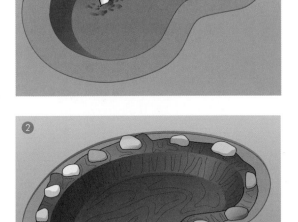

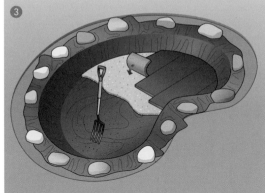

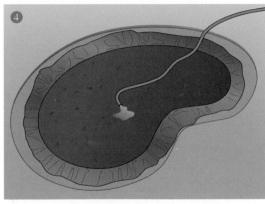

TOP-UPS AND OVERFLOWS

● Where water loss may be a problem, perhaps due to excessive evaporation during the summer months, a top-up system will help maintain a constant water level. A simple ball valve, of the type used for toilet cisterns, will allow the pond to be topped up automatically from an adjoining tank or pool, concealed by timber or a slab to support a plant container for disguise.

● Excess rainfall may cause some ponds to overflow, damaging the fabric of the banks. A pipe can be inserted into the side and set at a gradient of no less than 1:80 to run off any superfluous water into a nearby ditch or land drain.

Incorporating a simple overflow pipe will prevent ponds spilling over in wet weather.

▼ Design your pond to suit the garden and landscape around it. You can always add a personal touch, like this unusual sculpture by Janet Williams.

The *Designs*

The following fifteen inspirational designs have been deconstructed, recipe style, into their component parts to enable you to combine and create your dream water garden feature.

barrel *fountain*

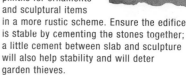

▶ **①** Stone slabs make great informal plinths for ornaments and sculptural items in a more rustic scheme. Ensure the edifice is stable by cementing the stones together; a little cement between slab and sculpture will also help stability and will deter garden thieves.

② Barrels are flexible enough to have many uses around the garden. Use them for planting as well as for water features, half hidden by foliage, which will help soften the effect. They can even be converted into garden seats and tables.

▶ **③** Cryptomeria japonica sinensis makes a frost-hardy cone of stiff branchlets, and is a popular cedar for Japanese gardens with many cultivars.

◀ **④** Juniperus is a slow-growing and long-lived evergreen—perfect for a permanent display in patio containers and pots. It has many forms and colors, including a tub-hugging prostrate cultivar, with the bonus of a pungent, spicy scent when brushed.

ADVANTAGES

● The whole arrangement takes up very little space and could be adapted to the tiniest backyard or patio.

● This easy-to-maintain area with its container-grown foliage looks good all year round and is easy to replace if you want a change or the plants get too big.

● The scheme is quick and easy to install, because everything is in containers, and could be taken with you should you move.

Using old barrels as ready-to-use raised ponds or planters creates an instantly mature, usually homespun, look to the backyard or patio. Here, however, barrels have been teamed with a humorous modern fountain sculpture and a billowing mass of year-round greenery to transform the tiniest corner into a sophisticated combination of stone, timber, and water.

The focal point of what was once a dull corner at the side of the house is a pair of rustic barrels, each with a floating "bather," the one spouting water onto the head of the other. They are observed by a large stone fish on a natural stone "plinth," and framed by massed evergreen plants to fill in the gaps. As a backdrop to the feature, a Japanese-style brushwood screen keeps the garbage cans concealed, and reinforces the distinctly oriental atmosphere that a limited use of color and a pleasing combination of natural materials have given this simple scheme. Certainly the effect of gently spilling water, strong foliage patterns, and well-weathered timber is very restful.

THE CAST OF CHARACTERS

▶ **⑤** False cypress (Chamaecyparis) is a useful conifer for containers, with its flattened branches and hardy nature. There is a good choice of cultivars with gold, blue, or bronze coloring.

▼ Euonymus fortunei is a shrubby creeper, ideal for softening the edges of tubs. Choose a compact cultivar with good variegated coloring, such as 'Emerald 'n' Gold' for year-round interest.

Juniperus horizontalis is a tough, cold-climate shrub perfect for containers with gray-green or blue foliage.

Common ivy (Hedera helix) is the ideal smotherer for walls, trellises, and containers. Frost-hardy, it thrives in shade, so is perfect for dark patio corners.

◀ Black bamboo (Phyllostachys nigra) makes a clump of slender canes that turn black once established and has long, narrow green leaves. It needs protection from cold winds.

▶ Persian ivy (Hedera colchica) is grown for its attractive heart-shaped leaves and its frost-hardy, fast-growing habit.

Other suggestions:

◀ Pretty maidenhair fern (Adiantum pedatum) is the hardiest of the species and prefers a cooler location. It produces lovely ferny fronds up to 2 feet (60 cm) long.

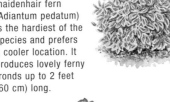

▲ Fatsia japonica makes a handsome shrub or small tree with exotic-looking palmate foliage. It is surprisingly hardy but dislikes direct sunshine. The flowers appear in fall.

◀ Coprosma includes ninety species of evergreen shrubs and small trees valued for their tolerance of salt winds in coastal areas. C. x kirkii has narrow, glossy leaves and is relatively frost-hardy.

▶ Common fig (Ficus carica) makes a small, deciduous, fruiting tree that enjoys being confined in a container and prefers a sunny position. It must be kept well watered or the fruit will split.

◀ Berberis is a large genus that includes many pretty evergreen forms with small leathery leaves and sharp spines.

▲ The smallest tub can be converted into a patio water garden complete with spouting ornament and miniature plants.

SETTING THE SCENE

BARRELS

Check if reclaimed barrels are watertight by filling with water. If it still leaks once the timber has swollen, the barrel needs to be lined with flexible liner attached to the inside top of the barrel with staples or nails. Alternatively, you can buy new barrels that have already been adapted to water features.

SCULPTURE

A piece of sculpture creates an instant focal point, especially in a courtyard or patio. Position it where it will create maximum effect: with a neutral background behind and softened by surrounding foliage. If you can't afford a professionally sculpted piece, invent your own using an old watering can, an ornate garden tap, or an ancient-looking urn, all of which can be easily converted into a water feature using a simple hose.

PLANTING

Dwarf or slow-growing evergreen shrubs make excellent container plants for low-maintenance patios or winter interest. Conifers and junipers are a classic choice and offer a fine selection of golds, grays and greens; but evergreen herbs, such as sage and rosemary, or small-leaved evergreens that can be clipped into formal shapes, such as box and privet, would look equally good.

BAMBOO SCREEN

Bamboo screens are available in many styles: from split bamboo canes arranged vertically or horizontally on a timber frame, to brushwood tied into bundles as used here. It has a much softer effect than traditional trellis and is useful for creating an oriental effect.

BEHIND THE SCENES

CREATING A BARREL FEATURE

Barrels make great mini water features that are quick and easy to create for the backyard or patio. If you are using a secondhand barrel, make sure it has been scrupulously cleaned out. Otherwise, yeast-forming residues will cause water-quality problems later.

① Check whether the barrels are watertight by filling with water and checking for leaks. If the staves aren't a tight fit you will have to line the barrel with flexible liner.

② Make a support ring for each barrel that will hold up the sculpture. Measure the length of water pipe required by fitting it into the barrel to make a tight fit about 6 inches (15 cm) from the top. Cut to length and join with a piece of dowelling to make a circle.

③ Fit the rings back into each barrel and drill holes in the pipe about 6 inches (15 cm) apart, taking care not to go right through both sides of the pipe.

④ Cut crossbars of dowel to length and fit them into the holes in a crisscross pattern for strength.

⑤ Remove the support ring from the barrels, then line them with flexible liner, pushing it right down into the corners.

⑥ Replace the support rings, pushing them down hard until they fit tightly. Fix the liner to the top of the barrel with galvanized nails. Trim away surplus liner with a sharp knife.

⑦ Arrange the pump in the lower barrel to the correct height. It may need propping up with a block or brick and tying in place with wire. Check that the barrel is level, and fill slowly with water. Add support ring.

⑧ Run the pump outlet pipe out over the back of the barrel and conceal behind a strategically placed plant or trelliswork. The cable to the electricity supply can be similarly hidden.

⑨ Position the head sculptures on the support rings, using bricks to adjust the height. Tie in place with wire if necessary.

⑩ Run the pipe behind the back of the taller barrel and push in at the back of the spouting head feature. Turn on the water and adjust the flow with the spray adjuster so that it pours into the lower barrel and onto the other feature without splashing.

POINTS TO REMEMBER

● Make sure you are happy with the position of your barrel (or barrels) before you fill them with water, because they will be too heavy to move when full.

● Underwater lighting will make an interesting feature of a barrel fountain after dark, but you will probably need a qualified electrician to arrange this for you.

① Check barrel is watertight

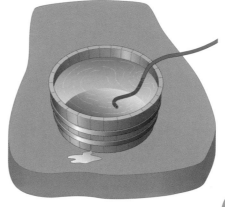

Euonymus fortunei

② Make support rings

③ Fit support rings

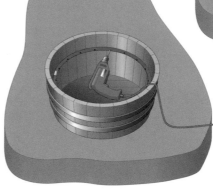

④ Cut and fit crossbars

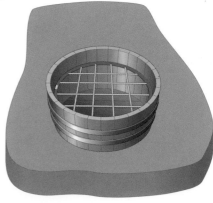

⑤ Remove rings and line barrels

⑥ Fit support ring in top barrel

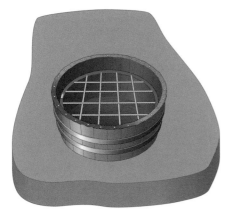

⑦ Put pump in lower barrel

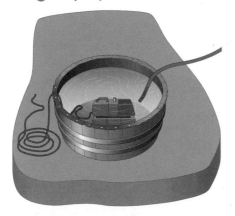

⑧ Position pump outlet

⑨ Place sculptures on supports

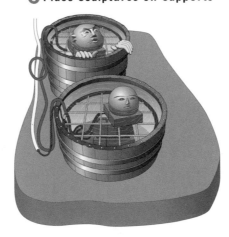

⑩ Fit water pipe into spout

▶ Linking a pair of barrels with a simple overspill of water may be drama enough in a corner of the patio.

Common fig

ADDITIONAL POINTS

● A low bubble or bell fountain would make a good alternative to a water spout, especially if you had room for only one barrel feature.

● Surrounding evergreens not only soften the edge of the barrels, they can also be used to conceal the water return pipe.

● Raising smaller sculptures and garden ornaments on a stone or timber plinth, like this fish, gives them more prominence, especially in densely planted areas.

● If you do not have room for two barrels, an ornamental head could be wall-mounted, spouting water into a single barrel below.

pebble *fountain*

▲ ❶ Hostas: Hosta fortunei 'Francee', H. decorata, H. sieboldiana 'Frances Williams'—designers' favorite foliage plants for water gardens, with their love of damp, shady places and large quilted leaves in a variety of colors.

ADVANTAGES

● Provided you lay weed-suppressing membrane beneath the gravel, this fountain is low-maintenance.

● A hidden reservoir makes this a water feature safe for use with young children.

● Although full of interest and different materials, it takes up very little space.

This gravel patio is small, but it beautifully combines different features and materials to make the perfect link between a more formal paved area and the rest of the garden, with the added interest of a small moving water feature. Much of its charm is a result of the harmonious juxtaposition of natural materials: timber, water, plants, and stone. With all the interest at ground level, strong foliage planting was important to screen the area from other parts of the garden and create a sense of seclusion.

In contrast to simple stone and timber, here is a rich variety of foliage shape and color—from lush hostas and grasses to the deeply cut leaves of an Acer palmatum in the background. Boulders among the plants forge a link with the gravel area in front and lead the eye down to the bubbling stone feature in its bed of pebbles. Since the sump is hidden underground, the focus is on the sound and movement of water.

For a change of texture, well-weathered railroad ties have been set into the gravel in a random design. Their roughness and earthy color make a good contrast with the smoothness of the surrounding stone and they double as an informal path.

▲ ❷ Seasoned timbers give a mature look to a feature with their rugged coloring and weathered appearance.

◄ ❸ Variegated grasses: Phalaris variegata with its striped leaves and white-striped Arrhenatherum bulbosum 'Variegatum' add lightness of color and form among more fleshy foliage.

THE CAST OF CHARACTERS

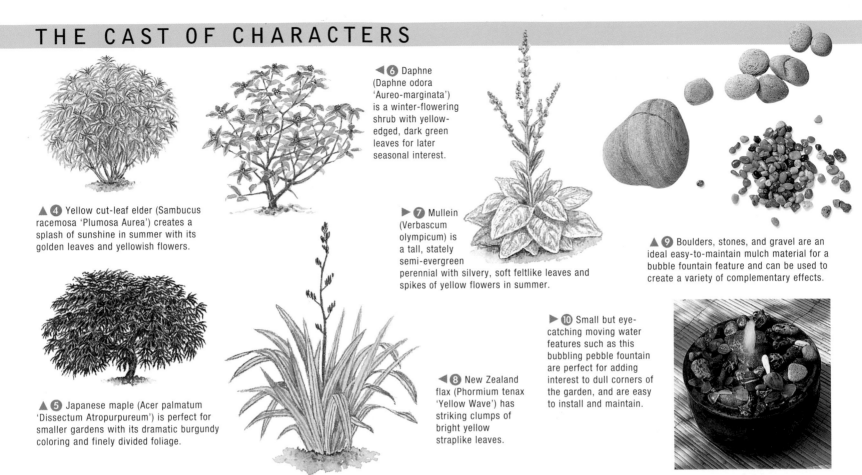

▲ ④ Yellow cut-leaf elder (Sambucus racemosa 'Plumosa Aurea') creates a splash of sunshine in summer with its golden leaves and yellowish flowers.

◄ ⑥ Daphne (Daphne odora 'Aureo-marginata') is a winter-flowering shrub with yellow-edged, dark green leaves for later seasonal interest.

► ⑦ Mullein (Verbascum olympicum) is a tall, stately semi-evergreen perennial with silvery, soft feltlike leaves and spikes of yellow flowers in summer.

▲ ⑨ Boulders, stones, and gravel are an ideal easy-to-maintain mulch material for a bubble fountain feature and can be used to create a variety of complementary effects.

▲ ⑤ Japanese maple (Acer palmatum 'Dissectum Atropurpureum') is perfect for smaller gardens with its dramatic burgundy coloring and finely divided foliage.

◄ ⑧ New Zealand flax (Phormium tenax 'Yellow Wave') has striking clumps of bright yellow straplike leaves.

► ⑩ Small but eye-catching moving water features such as this bubbling pebble fountain are perfect for adding interest to dull corners of the garden, and are easy to install and maintain.

SETTING THE SCENE

PEBBLE FOUNTAIN
Perfect for smaller gardens, these provide the pleasure of a moving water feature in the minimum of space. The water is recycled via an underground reservoir and bubbles up through large cobbles, a single large boulder, or an old millstone. Installation is simple and the possibilities above ground are endless: the water could bubble up out of any waterproof receptacle.

GRAVEL AREA
Laid on a weed-free membrane, an area of gravel looks good all year, requires virtually no maintenance, and can be used to set off other features and materials, particularly timber and water. The gravel comes in a variety of sizes and colors: mix it with colorful aquarium gravel for added sparkle and interest.

FOLIAGE
Selecting plants according to foliage shape and color can create interesting contrasts and harmonies. Within the spectrum of the fleshy leaves of the hostas, soft, velvet herbs and spiky grasses, there is also a rich tapestry of colors: the purples of sage and a flaming Japanese maple, Acer palmatum 'Dissectum' Atropurpureum .

RAILROAD TIES
Railroad ties can be purchased quite cheaply; they last well and create an old-fashioned effect. Set them in contrasting gravel for an interesting path or patio area. They also make excellent decking, pergolas, informal bridges, and pond edging. For a less rustic effect, substitute new timber and stain to the color of your choice.

BEHIND THE SCENES

INSTALLING A PEBBLE POND

Pebble ponds can be purchased in kit form or as individual components for creating your own look. Often the pond perimeters will be planted with lush plants such as ferns and hostas in pots or specially created planting beds. Changing the plants and pebbles can give your water feature a fresh new look.

1 Dig a hole as deep, but slightly wider, than your reservoir. Place the reservoir into position and backfill with sand to ensure a snug fit. Lay a spirit level across the rim to check the unit is level. Place a polythene sheet over the bog area, with a hole smaller than the diameter of the reservoir so water can flow back in from the edge.

2 Place a small pump into the reservoir, resting it on a brick to prevent any silt at the bottom of the pond from being sucked in.

3 Unless you are using a preformed reservoir with a slatted lid, cut a circle of wire mesh about 5 inches (12 cm) wider than the final pool size. Lay it over the reservoir and fasten it to the ground using wire staples. Cut a flap into the wire with wire-cutters for easy access to the pump. The fountain spout should protrude through a hole in the mesh.

4 Position a large predrilled rock—bought from a garden or aquatic center—over the spout, making sure the pipe fits into the hole.

5 Lay the pebbles across the mesh, starting at the outer rim and piling them up toward the middle for the best effect.

Hosta

POINTS TO REMEMBER

• Water loss through spray is inevitable, which means pondside plants will do well; regular filling is important to compensate for this.

• Larger, shallow pebble ponds will need to be lined with pond liner and gravel, pebbles or rocks laid carefully on top.

• Pump and sump will get silted up after a time. Make a point of dismantling yours and cleaning it out at least once a year to ensure that it runs smoothly.

1 Install the reservoir

2 Position the pump on a brick

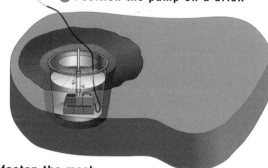

3 Lay and fasten the mesh

4 Position the main rock

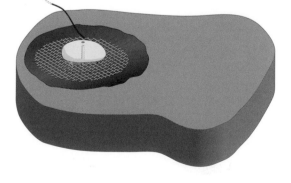

5 Place the pebbles over the mesh

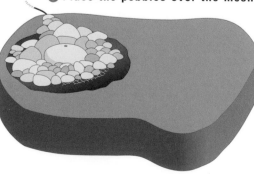

LAYING A GRAVEL AREA AND POSITIONING TIES

Whether your project involves a path or patio, gravel, stone, or pebbles, you will save yourself a lot of work if you prepare the site properly and invest in a weed-suppressing permeable membrane to lay beneath. Loose gravel needs a firm edge such as timber or curbstones to hold it in place.

① Clear weeds and debris from the site. Spray with weed killer. Prepare the base with a level foundation of 4 inches (10 cm) of rubble.

② Cover the area with a permeable membrane to allow water through but suppress the growth of weeds. Buy this by the yard or meter from garden centers and building supply stores.

③ Spread a 1 inch (2.5 cm) layer of gravel over the membrane, using a rubber-tined rake. To bed the timber railroad ties safely, use a level to ensure the ground is even.

④ Put down a 2 inch (5 cm) layer of sand, lay the tie on top, then fill in between with gravel.

▲ A series of drilled stones or concrete orbs among the pebbles make a exciting alternative fountain effect.

① Prepare the base

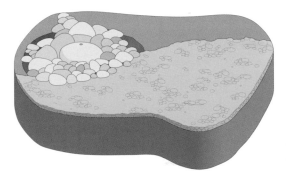

② Lay down the permeable membrane

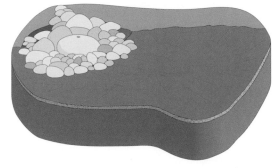

③ Spread gravel over the membrane

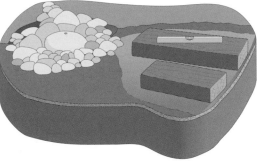

④ Position the railroad ties

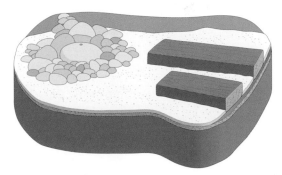

POINTS TO REMEMBER

● Gravel is usually sold by the cubic yard. To estimate how much you need, one cubic yard of gravel covers at least 24 square yards (20 sq. m) to a depth of 1 inch (2.5 cm).

● For a different finish, replace the gravel with small pebbles.

● If you are installing a pebble or gravel area close to the house, the final surface must be at least 6 inches (15 cm) below the damp-proof course, and have a slope of 1 in 100 away from the building to drain off rainwater.

Gravel and pebbles are available in a choice of sizes and colors.

ADDITIONAL POINTS

● The minimum size for a ground-level circular pebble pond is around 12 inches (30 cm) in diameter. Should you need to extend it, make sure the liner is big enough to reach beyond the size of the pond to ensure that any over-spray and drips drain back into the sump.

● If the feature is likely to freeze in winter, empty the sump before the first frosts, clean the pump, and store it in a dry shed or garage.

● Slug-prone plants like hostas could be grown in pots with a slug band or petroleum jelly around the base, tucked in among the other plants.

● Use only washed stone and gravel to prevent polluting the water in the sump. If using stones and boulders you have found around the garden, scrub with disinfectant solution, rinse, and dry before using.

informal koi
pond

▲ **❶** Fish such as koi add a new dimension to the pond and are worth the little extra care required for the design and entertainment potential they can offer.

❷ Rocks with good shapes and markings are worth paying extra for when they are the focal point of a feature like this one.

This enchanting yet modestly sized fishpond gives the impression of a lush jungle pool in a small but well-sheltered corner of the garden. Craggy rocks hang over the pond's edge and are built up behind to create an atmospheric backdrop. Any hard edges are softened by exotic-looking but often hardy plants such as rheum, grasses, and ferns. Their overlapping spikes, fronds, and parasols present a patchwork of green shades.

Any eye-catching splashes of brighter color are reserved for the flash of koi as they dart in and out of the shadows of the dark waters (see pages 134 to 135 on keeping koi). The clever combination of foliage shapes and sizes that fringe the pond not only help to transform a small, basic kidney-shaped pond into a small slice of "wilderness", but also provide something of interest all the year round, an opportunity to hide necessary pumps and filters, and useful shelter for the fish too.

Here is a design that manages to combine everything you might desire in a pond, yet in the minimum of space: an informal, almost wild feel, a dramatic display of plants, and the excitement and pleasure that fish—especially koi—can bring.

▲ Water fringe or yellow floating heart (Nymphoides peltata) is a hardy aquatic with heart-shaped, submerged leaves and bright golden flowers like miniature water lilies.

THE CAST OF CHARACTERS

▲ ❸ Water lily (Nymphaea marliacea 'Chromatella') is a vigorous, easy-to-grow water lily with yellow blooms.

▶ ❹ Curry plant (Helichrysum angustifolium) is a useful foliage plant with its silver-gray coloring and aromatic leaves.

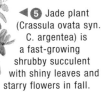

◀ ❺ Jade plant (Crassula ovata syn. C. argentea) is a fast-growing shrubby succulent with shiny leaves and starry flowers in fall.

▼ ❻ Male fern (Dryopteris filix-mas) will eventually form a large clump of attractive, green arching fronds.

▲ ❼ Common stonecrop (Sedum acre) is a hardy succulent that hugs tightly to rocks and produces a mass of yellow flowers in spring.

▲ ❽ Labrador violet (Viola labradorica) has been allowed to spread along the cracks in the edging and produces a display of mauve flowers in spring.

◀ ❾ Tiger aloe partridge-breasted aloe (Aloe variegata) makes a clump of boldly marked foliage with clusters of orange flowers in spring.

◀ ❿ Weigela praecox 'Variegata' is a deciduous shrub with attractive cream-striped foliage and star-shaped pink trumpet flowers.

▶ ⓫ Gunnera manicata makes a giant clump of huge 8 foot (2.4 m) wide leaves and thrives in boggy soil.

▲ ⓬ Marsh pennywort is a creeping bog plant with rounded, almost circular, leathery leaves. The flowers are insignificant. If you have a small pond, avoid using this plant.

◀ ⓭ Acorus gramineus is a small version of the sweet flag, with soft, curved leaves and pale green flower spikes.

SETTING THE SCENE

POND LINER
Preformed liners are readily available in informal shapes and, with careful fitting and edging, can look completely natural. Dark shades tend to be most popular, in particular black, which is less obtrusive, more resistant to UV light, and creates the impression of depth. Liners might be made of glass fiber or high-density polyethylene; the length of the guarantee (between 10 and 30 years) is a good indication of quality and UV resistance.

KOI
Koi are among the most popular ornamental pond fish, possibly because of their markings, tameness, and their potential size. They do require a little more care than their close relation, the goldfish, and the right food, clean, well-oxygenated water, and some winter care are essential to their health.

EDGING
Natural stone can make a superb edging to an informal pond, especially if the edge of the pond is steep. Drystone walling stone or large, flat stones are best for pond edging, although concrete reproduction paving stones or stepping-stones can be very realistic at less cost. The important thing is to hide any sign of the liner.

PLANTING
Keeping the scheme almost monochromatic has offered scope for contrasts between large fleshy leaves and tall, spiky subjects such as grasses, and helps create a suitably lush atmosphere around and on the water. Importantly, the plants have been allowed to intermingle and spread between the edging stones to encourage a sense of wild abundance.

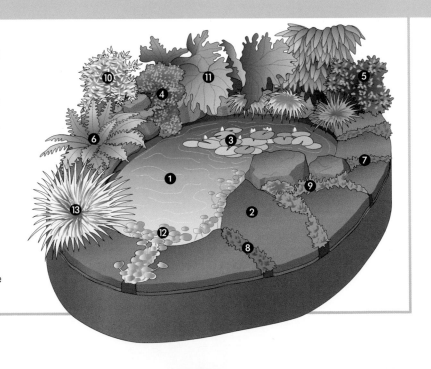

BEHIND THE SCENES

INSTALLING A PREFORMED POND

Molded ponds come in a wide range of shapes and sizes, from informal wildlife types to formal circles and squares. Some include a marginal shelf in the design; others even have facility for a pump and filter—a real asset for fish owners. Size is crucial too. Smaller, shallower pools heat up and cool down quickly, so they will be depleted of oxygen in summer and freeze in winter, and will not be suitable for keeping fish.

① Position the preformed pond on the ground, and make sure it looks right in relation to other features. Use canes and a piece of rope or hose to mark out the shape on the ground.

② Cut the outline of the pond with a sharp spade, allowing 6 inches (15 cm) for fitting and backfilling. Dig out the shape, and use a stick as a depth gauge to mark the position of the shelves and the depth of the pond. Allow 2 inches (5 cm) on the base for a layer of sand.

③ When the hole has been dug, check the bottom and sides for stones and sharp objects before spreading a 2 inch (5 cm) level layer of sand across the base.

④ Bed the pond into position, making sure it fits comfortably, and check its position and level with a batten and spirit level. Rake out the sand to adjust if necessary.

⑤ Once the pond is in position, fill it to about 4 inches (10 cm) with water to stabilize it. Check the levels again before backfilling with sand, tamping it down as you go. Work around the pond, slowly filling with water and checking the levels at every stage.

⑥ Use your hands to work the sand into position, especially under shelves and indentations, to make sure there are no air spaces. Once the shelves are supported, add water and check the levels again. Continue packing with sand and adding water until the pond is full.

POINTS TO REMEMBER

● To reduce the possibility of fish overheating in summer or freezing in winter, aim to select a pond that has a minimum depth of 18 inches (45 cm)—24 inches (60 cm) in colder areas—and a minimum surface area of 40 square feet ft (4 sq m).

● When choosing a preformed pond, check whether it will fit into your car or trailer as well as into the garden. Does your supplier offer a delivery service, and at what cost?

● Install any necessary pipework and electrical wiring before you put in your edging stones or slabs so that they can be hidden beneath. Tucking them into a metal or plastic conduit will help to minimize damage.

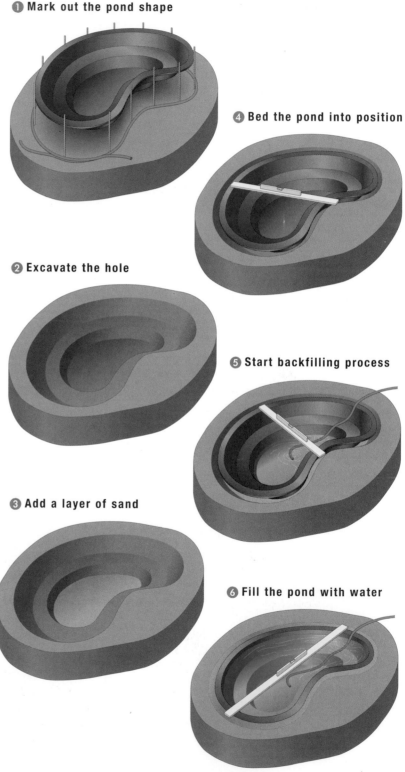

① Mark out the pond shape

② Excavate the hole

③ Add a layer of sand

④ Bed the pond into position

⑤ Start backfilling process

⑥ Fill the pond with water

LAYING ROCK PAVING AROUND THE POND

Nothing looks worse than liner showing around your pond; stone slabs are a good disguise. They can be be laid to overlap the pond edge slightly so that, even if the water level drops, the liner is still hidden. This may seem like a quick job, but your patience will be rewarded with a more natural and pleasing effect.

1 For a natural look, make sure you lay the stones securely with their strata lines all facing in the same direction. It helps if you have more slabs than you need, so you can choose the best combination. Lay out all the slabs before fixing, then stand back to survey the effect.

2 When you are satisfied that each slab is in the right position, fix them with a 1 to 2 inch layer of 5:1 sand: cement mortar.

3 You can fill any gaps between uneven shapes with loose, small pieces of stone or pebbles by pressing them into the mortar while it is still wet. Or insert plants in some of the spaces between the slabs: tamp down topsoil instead of mortar between the slabs and add plants while they are still small. Water them regularly until they are established.

◀ There are as many edging options for ponds as there are styles of paving. Here, a level arrangement of random slabs produces a semi-informal feel, and helps obscure the pond liner.

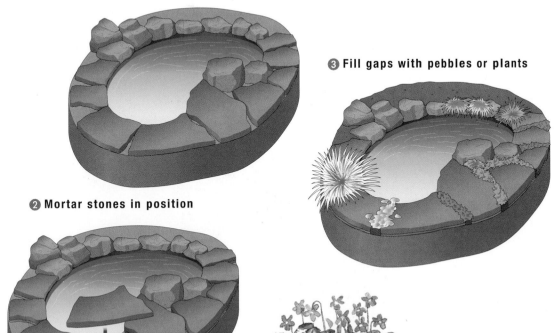

1 Lay stones out before fixing

2 Mortar stones in position

3 Fill gaps with pebbles or plants

Labrador violet

POINTS TO REMEMBER

● If you intend to finish the edge of the pond with flat stones or slabs, take their thickness into account when calculating the depth of your excavation, so that they can lie flush with the surrounding ground. Start paving with the thickest slabs.

● Work out in advance how you are going to move heavy stones or slabs. You may need a crane or winch to position them over the garden fence, and the use of a strong wheelbarrow to transport them to the side of the pond.

● Don't try and fix stones in position on extremely wet days or if there is any threat of frost.

ADDITIONAL POINTS

● Careful choice of planting can create a most definite look, like this exotic combination of dramatic foliage shapes, even though the plants themselves are not particularly tender.

● The beauty of using leaf shape and color as the basis of your design is that the pond can look good all year round—important if your garden is small or the pond is visible from the house or the conservatory.

● Sandstone and limestone are good materials for edging a pond, and a local stone is usually an inexpensive option. The more pronounced the markings, the more rugged the look.

● Buying stone locally is cheaper and reduces transport costs. Local quarries should be able to offer a good choice of different types in a wide range of prices.

1 Small rocky falls add movement to the pond without dominating the feature. A small pump positioned in the main pond is sufficient to run a feature like this; alternatively, you can use the same pump that powers the pond filters, if it has sufficient capacity.

▲ **2** A pebble beach incorporated in an informal pond design provides a useful change of texture and picks up on the oriental flavor of the ornaments.

oriental *accent*

ADVANTAGES

- Adds movement and interest to a large featureless area of the garden.

- Combines various elements within a unified scheme.

- Looks interesting and attractive from all angles.

Acer palmatum atropurpureum provides shape and color.

Garden designer Julian Treyer-Evans has created an oasis of movement and color with his design incorporating a large pond, bog garden, cascade, planting beds, and pebble area as a single organic unit within a green ocean of lawn. Central to the feature is the kidney-shaped pond, complete with small cascading falls, fish, and water lilies, extended into a pebble beach at one end.

On the far side, the pond blends seamlessly into a boldly planted bog garden, which is mirrored on the opposite bank by planting beds of conifers and evergreens, making a patchwork of golds and greens for all-year interest, right up to the water's edge.

The finishing touch to this informal yet immaculately maintained water garden complex is a selection of strategically positioned ornamental features: a tall pagoda and a pair of bronze cranes whose oriental elegance add height and interest to the pondside planting beds. The overall impression is one of calm and order, despite the exuberance of dramatic bog plants and the soothing splash of the cascade, which bubbles up—seemingly spontaneously—among the pondside boulders and tumbles gently into the pool.

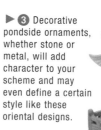

▶ **3** Decorative pondside ornaments, whether stone or metal, will add character to your scheme and may even define a certain style like these oriental designs.

4 Acer palmatum dissectum is a smaller cultivar of the showy Japanese maple, with deeply cut foliage and good color in fall.

5 Hosta sieboldiana is prized for its large, blue-shaded foliage; left alone, it will make a large clump after several years.

◀ **6** Rodgersia is a moisture-loving bog plant useful for its bold foliage and late summer plumes of flowers.

THE CAST OF CHARACTERS

◀ **7** Bear's breeches (Acanthus) is frost-hardy and prefers a rich, moist soil. The dramatic, deeply toothed leaves and large, strange flower spikes make very distinctive plumes of flowers.

▼ **8** Taxus baccata, the Common yew, with its dense, dark green foliage is a good foil for other trees.

▲ **9** Carex elata 'Aurea' is a grass with fine foliage and bright golden coloring, and is ideal for moist soils and bog gardens.

▲ **10** Viburnum davidii is a Chinese evergreen that makes a dense shrub with glossy, oval leaves and white flowers in spring, followed by blue berries.

▲ **11** Berberis thunbergii 'Atropurpurea' has rounded leaves with a deep purple and brown coloring that turn almost black in winter.

▼ **12** Spiraea 'Gold Mound' makes a dense clump of wiry shoots, covered in golden, narrow leaves.

▲ **13** American skunk cabbage (Lysichiton americanus) is a distinctive sight at the waterside in spring, with its large yellow spathes, followed by bright green foliage.

▲ **14** Marsh marigold (Caltha palustris) makes a fine display of shiny yellow, buttercuplike flowers in spring above dark green leaves.

▼ **15** Cedrus deodara 'Aurea' is a quick-growing cultivar of the cedar with golden branch tips, that reach 30 feet (9 m) in only ten years.

▶ **17** Juniperus chinensis 'Pfitz. Old Gold' adds a splash of color with its gold foliage and can be a welcome wind break.

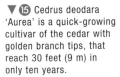

◀ **16** Corylus avellana 'Contorta' has elaborately twisted branches that provide winter interest.

◀ **18** Paeonia lactiflora is a beautiful hybrid paeony with fragrant white to yellow blooms.

▶ **19** Glyceria maxima 'Variegata' is a handsome ornamental grass with cream or white striped foliage.

SETTING THE SCENE

SUNKEN POND

The pond is informal but sparkling clear, thanks to an efficient system of filters—important if it is to provide a contrast to the surrounding lawns and planting. One of the delights of owning pond like this is its light-reflecting qualities and the reflections of surrounding planting and overhead clouds.

ISLAND BEDS

The planting in the surrounding beds is colorful and permanent: a clever blend of shrubs and evergreens that keep this feature looking good all year round. Positioning evergreens close to water minimizes leaf drop too, and keeps maintenance to a minimum.

LAWNS

An immaculately kept lawn sweeping around the garden makes the perfect background for a sunken pond, as long as clippings and chemical grass treatments are kept out of the water. Here planting beds and pebbles are a logical barrier between lawn and pond, and make mowing easier too.

FISH

Fish add life, color, and movement to a pond, but you must arrange sufficient filtration to deal with the fish waste. Here the pond is big enough to support fish, lilies, and a small cascade. The moving water is a useful source of oxygen for the fish, but needs to be kept clear of the water lilies, because such movement damages the foliage.

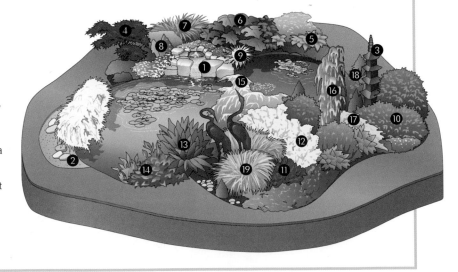

BEHIND THE SCENES

BUILDING A LARGE INFORMAL POND

A large informal pond will transform a blank stretch of lawn and be far less work to maintain. With a blank canvas like this and no other features to landscape to, the most natural-looking effect will be achieved with gentle sinuous curves and a loose egg-timer or kidney shape. Careful planting will help give the pond a more mature look and will link it with surrounding beds and borders

❶ Mark out the shape of the total feature, including planting beds and shingle area, using a hose or canes and string. View it from as many angles as possible—even from an upstairs window. When you are satisfied, strip back the turf using a turfing spade; roll soil side out and keep moist for use later.

❷ Excavate the pool area with a mechanical digger, allowing for layers of rubble and cement. Dig the bog area to a depth of around 2 feet (60 cm). Finish shaping and firming by hand with a spade. Spread over a 2-inch (5-cm) layer of sand.

❸ Put down a 4-inch (10-cm) layer of compacted rubble. Build up the sides by cementing blocks or bricks to the required height. Stagger the joins for strength and add a water-proofer to the 4:1 cement mix.

❹ Render the inside of the pond with a trowel and a 4:1 mix of cement mortar with added waterproofer. Overlap the edge of the pond by 6 inches (15 cm) for a neat finish. Leave to harden.

❺ Leave for three weeks to weather the lime in the cement and avoid polluting the water. You can then fill the pond slowly with a hose.

❻ To make the cascade, line the proposed area with a piece of flexible liner (this could be continued from the bog area), allowing it to come down at the front into the pond.

❼ Cement cascade boulders together (apart from side boulders and stones facing the inside of the pond). You will need a wide flat-topped stone set slightly lower than the others to allow the water to spill over into the pond.

❽ Set a piece of flat slate in the middle of the rocks with a hole bored in the center, and run a pipe under and up through the hole. Keep in place with bricks around the edges of the liner.

❾ Insert the other end of the pipe into the main pond, concealing it behind the boulders and lush bog plants. This can be connected to a submersible pump beneath the water in the main pond.

❿ When the pond and other features are completed, roll back the turf to hide the edges of the liner and plant up the planting beds.

❶ Mark out shape of whole feature

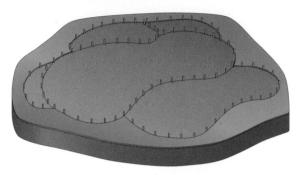

❷ Excavate the pond and bog areas

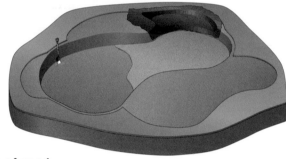

❹ Render inside of pond

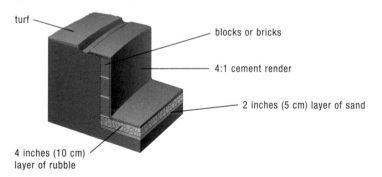

turf

blocks or bricks

4:1 cement render

2 inches (5 cm) layer of sand

4 inches (10 cm) layer of rubble

❸ Add rubble and build wall

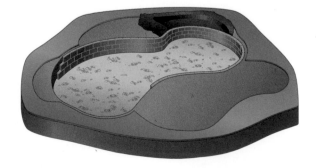

❺ Leave for three weeks, then fill

6 Line cascade area with liner

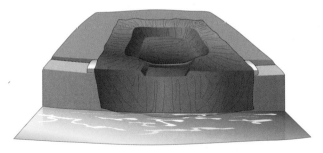

7 Cement cascade stones together

8 Insert water pipe through slate hole

9 Run pipe into pond and attach to pump

▲ An oriental pagoda sets the scene for a combination of bamboo, gravel, and stepping stones around this pond.

10 Replace turf to hide liner

American skunk cabbage

POINTS TO REMEMBER

● When creating the initial shape, avoid any narrow necks or tight curves. They will make it difficult to line, and may also encourage stagnant areas.

● For large ponds, excavate with the help of a mechanical digger. They can be rented by the day or the weekend, and will save you weeks of work.

● Before work starts, plan how to dispose of the spoil from digging the pond. You could use it to landscape another part of the garden. Or you could rent a suitably sized refuse container. Remember, soil bulks up by 50 percent once it is excavated.

● Positioning the bog garden immediately flanking the pond not only looks completely natural, but can also make a useful overflow facility in excessively wet weather.

● Always check that ornaments are fully weatherproof before leaving them out in the garden all year round.

grotto with fish spouts

The soft shield fern, Polystichum setiferum, has handsome bipinnate fronds up to 4 feet (1.2 m) long.

A moving water feature makes a fine focal point, but this trio of fish spouts in a small pool has taken that concept to its zenith in its setting of a theatrical grotto in a semicircular alcove. The classical grotto has been popular since Roman times and was especially loved by the Victorians, who had a passion for anything with Gothic overtones.

This contemporary version uses dressed blocks of reconstituted stone; its creamy, smooth finish makes a dramatic contrast with the rough, rocky back wall. The grotto features three stone fish with spouts—each symmetrically positioned to maximize the feature's dramatic impact—and the whole display is illuminated by concealed uplighters.

The wide stone slabs that make up the pool's sill double as a seat from which to admire the moving water show and the pleasing mix of rock, water, and greenery; even the container plants that flank the front of the pool are matching topiary pyramids. This is a stunning feature for a patio, but it would also look good in a corner of the garden, or even indoors among exotic plants in a large conservatory.

▲ ❶ Ferns: the delicate fronds of lady fern (Athyrium filix-femina), the large soft shield fern (Polystichum setiferum), and adder's fern (Polypodium vulgare)—with its evergreen crested fronds—are perfect for suggesting the dark, damp, mysterious atmosphere of a grotto.

◄ ❷ Topiary: clipped box (Buxus sempervirens) is used to create matching ornamental features in the pots fronting the pond.

THE CAST OF CHARACTERS

▲ **3** A decorative wall in dressed stone, wilder random boulders, or more formal brickwork will set the scene for a grotto.

4 Wide copings make an attractive edging to the feature and double as a place to sit and observe the water.

▶ **5** Greater pond sedge (Carex riparia) thrives in waterlogged areas such as bogs and swamps.

▼ **6** Hosta (Hosta fortunei 'Aurea Marginata') makes a dramatic foliage display with its classic broad-pleated leaves, edged in yellow.

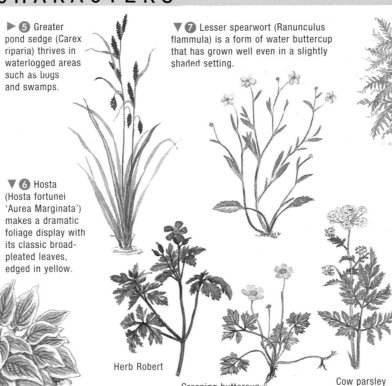

▼ **7** Lesser spearwort (Ranunculus flammula) is a form of water buttercup that has grown well even in a slightly shaded setting.

Herb Robert

Creeping buttercup

Cow parsley

▲ **8** Self-seeded weeds—such as wild creeping buttercup, cow parsley, and herb Robert—help to give the grotto a slightly wild, abandoned look.

◀ **9** Royal fern (Osmunda regalis) is the largest of the species with its huge, feathery fronds and attractive golden coloring in fall.

▼ **10** An ornamental spout such as a head, fish, dolphin, or classical feature is essential when creating a semiformal grotto such as this, and is easily installed.

SETTING THE SCENE

STONE GROTTO

The beauty of a grotto is the dramatic effect it provides in a relatively small space. It has height and depth, but need not be large, especially if you add lighting and the sight and sound of running water. This ready-made theatrical alcove is available in sections, but you could easily build your own garden grotto using old bricks, slabs, crazy paving, or rough stone. The important thing to remember is to fit all the pipes and electrical work before you complete the construction.

SPOUTS

A fountain or spout is highly decorative yet easy to install, making it a perfect feature for small spaces where moving water might inject a little excitement. You don't have to build an elaborate grotto—choose a simple old garden tap dripping into a bowl on the back wall of the patio, or a decorative sculpted head or bronze lizard spouting water into an ornamental trough. Garden centers and artists offer a good range.

LIGHTING

Lighting adds a new dimension to a patio or garden. Use it to highlight specific features or as part of a more general scheme to lighten the garden after dark. A wide range of fixtures is available for outdoor use, including uplighters, spotlights, and low-voltage underwater lights. Lighting alongside paths, drives, and bridges is an important safety measure, as well as looking good. Employ a qualified electrician to complete the fitting, for safety's sake. Keep your domestic and outdoor power supplies separate, so the outdoor supply can't trigger the domestic trip switch.

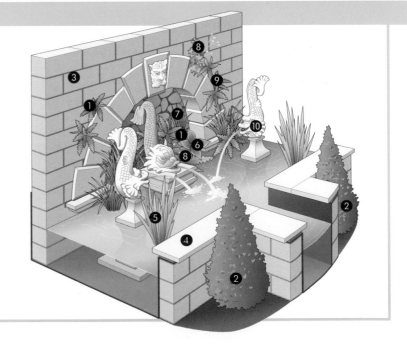

BEHIND THE SCENES

BUILDING A GROTTO

A stony grotto creates a wonderful surprise water feature in the garden, or the conversation point of a patio. If you are building it yourself, it can be as grand or Gothic as you choose.

▶ For a more informal feature, a simple spouting head can be fixed to a rough wall and partially concealed by ferns.

① Build your wall on top of the pond liner to the height and width you require, using bricks, or dressed or random stone.

② Construct two pillars to the front of the wall to the width and height of your proposed alcove.

③ Take a piece of plywood and bend it over from pillar to pillar to create an arch. Cement a brick or stone to the top of each pillar to hold the timber in place.

④ Continue with the brick or stonework up and over to create the arched effect. The middle top stone (the keystone) is the last to be fitted, as it locks all the stones into place. When this is done, gently draw out the plywood, cutting it if necessary. Point up for a neat finish, or leave random stones more craggy for a less formal effect.

Shield fern

② Construct pillars on each side

④ Complete the stonework

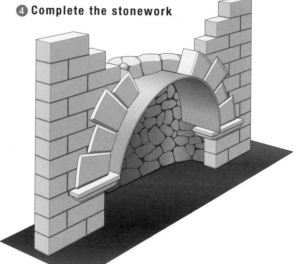

① Build the back wall of the grotto

③ Make the arch with plywood and bricks

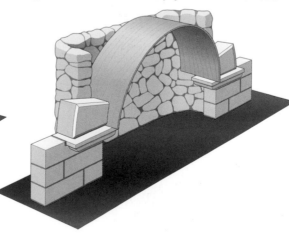

POINTS TO REMEMBER

● The back wall of the grotto can be carried on beyond the width of the alcove to create a larger backdrop to the pond.

● If you are planning to light your grotto, make room for the cables during construction. Consult an electrician before work starts.

● Plumbing should also be allowed for during construction if a water spout is going to be incorporated.

INSTALLING WATER FEATURES IN THE POND

The sound and sight of moving water adds life and movement to a feature, yet it is very easy to install. The water can be recycled via an ornamental pool, basin, or trough sited below.

1 Place concrete slabs on the liner—larger than the base of each fish feature—and position the fish on top of the slabs.

2 Submerge a low-voltage pump into the pool and place it on top of the pool lining.

3 Attach a three-way hose adaptor to the outlet of the pump.

4 Attach three flexible water supply pipes to the adaptor, making sure the pipes are long enough to reach the water features. Push the ends of the flexible pipes onto the spouts of the three features.

5 Use a clamp to adjust the water flow to each feature.

1 Position the water features

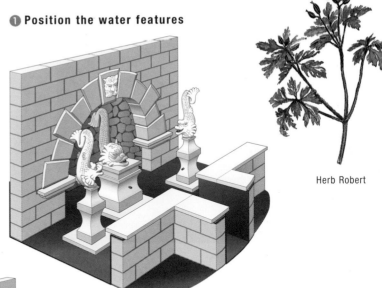

Herb Robert

2 Install the pump

POINTS TO REMEMBER

● You will need to run a power supply via a transformer to the pump from an electrical power source plug fitted with a circuit breaker.

● The electricity cable can be concealed underneath the coping of a wall or buried 18 inches (46 cm) below a flowerbed, whichever is convenient.

● Protect electricity cable in the garden with a pipe or conduit to prevent accidentally slicing through it with a spade. Make sure you use armored cable.

Only use waterproof connectors recommended for outdoor use.

4 Connect the hose and features

3 Attach a hose adaptor to the pump

5 Adjust the water flow

ADDITIONAL POINTS

● Use plants to soften your feature: pots of hostas around the pool at the base and ivies or other climbers smothering the wall behind will do much to enhance the overall appearance of the grotto and will give it a more mature look.

● Stone and terracotta classical masks—or even the lighter plastic or fiber glass versions that are now available from garden centers—can be a simple yet effective outlet for a water spout.

● For a different effect, face the grotto with shells or small colored stones; or even try ceramic tiles and mosaic for a more Mediterranean look.

● Unless you want to cultivate a well-weathered, half-neglected feel to the feature, give the stone an annual rub-down and rinse it with a wire brush to remove moss and algae growth.

❶ Stepping-stones provide access across grass or gravel as well as water, and are available as preshaped pieces from major paving companies. Lay flush in the grass to aid easy mowing.

▲ **❷** A paved area—whether slabs, crazy paving, or decking—can link a pond with the rest of the garden, and need not be close by the house. Position it where it will receive the most sunshine. Paved pond edging hides the liner and makes mowing the lawn to the water's edge easier.

informal pond and falls

ADVANTAGES

● All-round access makes this an easy feature to maintain.

● Creates a focal point to be enjoyed from the house and the rest of the garden.

● Combines many features: patio, plants, pool, fish, falls, and rockery.

Your pond will soon be populated by many fascinating underwater and airborne insect visitors.

When working with a blank canvas like this new house plot, you need a major feature to act as a starting point for your design. Here a charming informal pool has been positioned across the far corner of the garden to avoid a squared-off look, creating a marvelous focal point that can be enjoyed from several angles

The pond may be informal, but it retains a clean, crisp look set in an emerald carpet of lawn with a well-groomed crazy paving patio to match the pond edging. Linking these hard landscaping features to the rest of the garden is a curve of stepping stones across the lawn that echoes the shape of the pond.

To add height to the pond feature and help disguise the garden boundaries further, a rockery has been built, which incorporates a series of small falls for the added pleasure of moving water. Carefully selected boulders make a fine contrast and are softened by clever all-year planting. Various conifers create mounds and pyramids of individual color, and spiky iris continues the watery theme up the rocks, a reflection of the reeds and rushes below. Even the water's surface is well-planted providing plenty of cover for the fish, but with an area left free for a summer display of water lilies.

▲ **❸** Falls, even of a modest size, make an excellent backdrop to a pond, and offer the sound and sight of moving water for the cost of a small pump.

THE CAST OF CHARACTERS

▶ **4** Pickerel weed (Pontederia cordata) is a pretty waterside plant with its pointed leaves and unusual blue flower spikes.

◀ **5** Parrot Feather (Myriophyllum aquticum syn. Myriophyllum proserpinacoides) has partly submerged feathery plumes with blue/green/yellow coloring.

▶ **6** Iris (Iris laevigata 'Variegata') will grow in sun or partial shade, where its striped, spiky foliage has a lightening effect.

▶ **7** Water mint (Mentha aquatica) is a pond-edge plant with aromatic foliage and lilac flowers from late summer to late fall.

◀ **8** Japanese arrowhead, Swamp potato (Sagittaria sagittifolia) has highly ornamental arrow-shaped flowers and showy flowers in summer.

▲ **9** Bog arum (Calla palustris) thrives in boggy soil, where it produces clumps of dark green, glossy leaves, and arum-like flowers followed by clusters of red berries.

▼ **10** Water lilies: Nymphaea Marliacea 'Carnea' with its star-shaped flowers held above floating leaves on strong stems, and free-flowering Nymphaea Marliacea 'Chromatella', highlight the pond surface in summer.

▼ **11** Conifers— including the golden Thuja orientalis 'Aurea'; the conical Sawara cypress, Chamaecyparis pisifera 'Boulevard', with its blue/green coloring; dwarf, silver-blue Juniperus communis 'Compressa', and golden Chamaecyparis 'Fletcheri'—create a rich backdrop of varying heights and colors.

▲ **12** Climbing Roses: Rosa 'Compassion' makes a colorful coverup in summer.

▲ **13** Alpines soften the base of the rockery: thyme, small Euphorbia, Crocosmia masonorum (shown above), and Echeveria.

SETTING THE SCENE

POND
To get the shape and position right, it is a good idea to experiment with a length of rope or hose before you start digging. When you have laid out your proposed shape, try to view it from all angles. Once you are satisfied, use the excavated soil to help build up the area behind to create the basis of a backdrop.

ROCKS
Rock and stone make useful contrasts of shape and texture in the garden and combine well with water. When tackling a rockery, the stonework needs to be chosen and positioned with care if it is to look natural. Try to use local stone wherever possible—with lower delivery costs, this will be cheaper to buy too—and lay according to its natural strata. Pockets of soil between the stones enable plants to be positioned between them, and soften their outline.

LAWN
A fine stretch of lawn can be one of the most splendid settings for an in-ground pond, providing it is in good condition and does not go right to the water's edge. Provide a ground-level edging of stone or slabs to prevent grass cuttings from polluting the water. Also beware of using lawn feeds and weed killers where runoff is likely to enter the pond. Stepping-stones or an informal path are important for providing dry access to the pond area in wet weather.

PATIO
Position your patio wherever you like in the garden if it means it will receive more sunshine. Incorporating it with another feature helps it to make sense, like here, where it is a continuation of the pond edging. Crazy paving has an informal look, but a pattern of slabs or pavers could be equally effective.

BEHIND THE SCENES

EDGING A POND WITH PAVING

Paving—whether random, irregular slabs or unit paving like bricks, slabs, or setts—makes a neat, attractive edging to a pond, perfect for disguising the liner and providing a dry, practical surface underfoot. It is important to prepare the site properly, ensuring that the foundations are stable. Crumbly soil will need to be replaced by rubble (broken bricks, concrete, or stones).

❶ Lay a good foundation of rubble about 4 inches (10 cm) deep.

❷ If you are using bricks or small cobblestone-type pavers, increase the layer to 6 inches (15 cm); these have a smaller surface area to take the weight of people walking on them.

❸ Position the broken flagstones or slabs around the pond, so that they follow the pond contours. When the design looks right, lay the stones or slabs onto a 1-inch (2.5-cm) bed of 3:1 sand and cement mix.

❹ Overlap the stones or slabs slightly over the edge of the pond to ensure that the liner is completely hidden. When they are level and neatly positioned around the pond, tamp them firmly into place.

❺ Use smaller slabs to fill in the spaces between the larger slabs, securing them with almost dry mortar. Bevel with a trowel for drainage. Leave to set for several days without walking on the slabs.

POINTS TO REMEMBER

● Check the level at every stage, using a spirit level, and double-check each slab individually after laying.

● Make sure that the total paved area slopes slightly back from the water to avoid unwanted runoff into the pond.

● Allow for the combined depth of all your foundation levels when excavating the area, so that the finished level is flush with the water's surface.

❶ **Lay a foundation of hardcore**

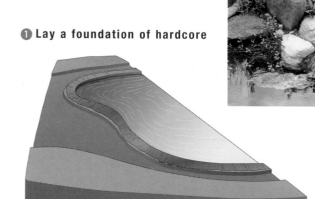

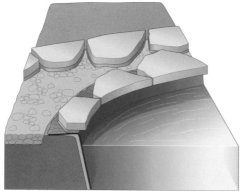

▲ You could even recreate a rocky mountain stream in your backyard.

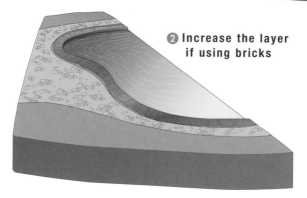

❷ **Increase the layer if using bricks**

❹ **Ensure stones overlap the edge**

❸ **Position the flagstones**

❺ **Fill in between the slabs**

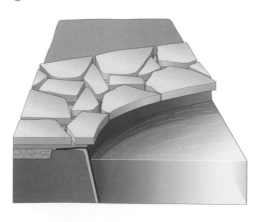

CREATING A ROCKERY WITH FALLS

A rockery makes an excellent backdrop for an informal pond: it makes good use of excavated soil, adds height to the feature, and offers the opportunity to grow a selection of alpine-type plants. Rocks can be purchased from garden and landscaping centers, but larger stones are better acquired from a local quarry. Always check cost of delivery and access to your garden. You will need them to be deposited as close to the site of your proposed rockery as possible.

❶ Build up an area behind the pond

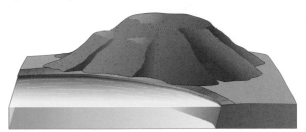

❷ Dig and shape the cascade

❸ Lay down liner and secure

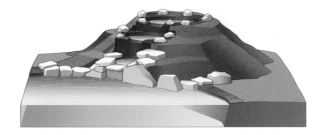

❹ Bed the stones on top

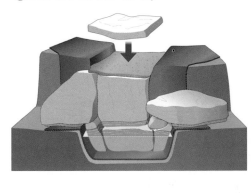

❺ Backfill spaces and fill with plants

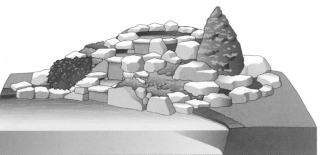

---

❶ Build up an area behind the pond to a height that is in proportion to your water project. Use the soil from your pond excavation to build the foundations. The mound should be left to settle for a few months; you will need to check that it is stable.

❷ When you've planned your cascade, dig and shape it until it looks right from all angles. Remove small stones and sharp objects, and cover it with a 1-inch (2.5-cm) layer of sand and/or underlay.

❸ Lay down a section of flexible liner over the course of the cascade to run right down into the pool; press it into position.

❹ Bed the stones on top, making sure that their strata run the same way for the most natural effect. If you feel the boulders need more stability, cement them to the liner with a stiff mortar mix. With the rocks at the side, about two-thirds of a boulder's bulk should be dug into the bank for stability and authenticity.

❺ Backfill the spaces between the stones with free-draining compost, and fill these crevices with suitable plants. Water regularly until the plants are established.

POINTS TO REMEMBER

● When planning and choosing plants, make sure you have something of interest for all seasons: many alpine plants are at their best in spring and summer, but dwarf conifers, heathers, and bulbs are useful for winter and fall displays.

● Consider the edges of your rockery feature and graduate them into the rest of the garden. Do not allow them to come to an abrupt end.

● Do you need access to the rockery from behind for maintenance? If so, do not position it too close to a boundary fence or trellis.

● Preformed cascades are ideal for smaller falls and save a lot of shaping and lining. They are available in a choice of shapes and sizes, but do need disguising with rocks and plants to look natural.

stream garden

A natural feature will attract a wide range of insects—even butterflies—if you choose good nectar plants.

A classical figurative sculpture is the focal point of this informal stream, where good underlying design and thoughtful planting have created a rich and varied water garden in a surprisingly small space. An awkward sloping site has been turned into an advantage by installing a natural-looking stream that cascades down the incline in a series of weirs. Mature planting of shrubs and plants partially hide the stream and the stony steps and path that run alongside it, giving the impression of a natural woodland walk.

A large rhododendron at the top of the bank helps to reinforce that look, but in reality path and stream lead nowhere: it is an optical illusion, and the elegant statue that draws your eye upward is nothing more than a lure.

It is such a delightfully wild, secluded area that these limitations don't seem to matter. It is enough to be drawn by the sound of water to discover the charming contrast created by the formal statue and the little wild stream with its overgrown plants and secret pool.

▲ ❶ The ostrich feather fern (Matteuccia struthiopteris) grows quickly to produce tall feathery plumes.

◀ ❷ Iris are popular poolside subjects with their elegant clumps of swordlike leaves and exotic, colorful flowers.

▶ ❸ St. John's wort (Hypericum) is grown for its long-lived mass of golden flowers among shrubby foliage.

◀ ❹ Camellias are beautiful evergreen flowering shrubs, with a choice of white, pink, or red blooms.

THE CAST OF CHARACTERS

▼ **5** Azalea (Azalea kaempferi) is a tall, frost-hardy shrub with blue/green foliage and spectacular wide-open, white flowers in the summer.

6 A stream: whether lined or created using preformed sections, a series of weirs and a slightly winding course creates the most natural effect.

▼ **7** A sculpture in a water garden is useful for creating a focal point and drawing the eye toward a more distant vista.

9 Campion (Lychnis) with its pretty summer flowers of white, pink, orange, or red, creates a suitably informal effect at the streamside.

▶ **8** Steps or a path following the course of a stream not only provide access to other parts of the garden, but will also allow you to observe streamside plants more closely.

▶ Broom (Genista) prefers a sunny site and a well-drained soil to produce a mass of scented pealike flowers.

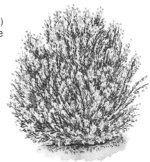

SETTING THE SCENE

STREAM
A stream is a great way to include a water feature into your garden without the excavation and commitment of a pond. It can meander around other features, be used as a linking device, and travel downhill. However, a man-made stream should be on level ground so that the water does not run to the lower level faster than the pump can return it. The solution for a sloping site is to build in a series of weirs that have to fill up and spill out before moving on.

PLANTING
Streams offer some wonderful planting opportunities: primulas, iris, rushes, or reeds allow infinite scope of shape and color for spring and summer interest. Shrubs and trees produce a display later in the year, and ferns and ivies recreate a lush streamside atmosphere.

SCULPTURE
The right ornament or sculpture can change the whole emphasis of your garden. As with any other art form, choice and style are a matter of personal taste, but the right position is important. Smaller items may need to be displayed on a shelf or plinth to bring them up to eye level; most need a suitable backdrop of a plain wall.

STONE PATH
A garden path is not just a means of getting from A to B without getting your feet wet. Well designed and installed, it can be an attractive feature in its own right: constructed in timber, stone, or gravel, it can provide contrasts of texture with other features, divide the garden into new areas, and metamorphose when required into stepping stones, bridges, and steps.

BEHIND THE SCENES

INSTALLING A SERIES OF WEIRS

Weirs not only help a stream cope with a change of level, but also add sparkle and interest to the garden, and the pleasant sound of water spilling from one ledge to the next. They are sometimes used to link two pools of different heights on a patio or lawn.

❶ Excavate the stream, base pond, and weirs out of a sloping site, and use the excavated soil to build up and landscape the area around the weirs. Keep to one side the top 6 inches (15 cm) of soil for planting.

❷ Check the base for stones and sharp objects, line the stream area with a 1-inch (2.5-cm) layer of sand to keep the ground level, and cover any remaining sharp objects.

❸ Lay flexible underliner over the stream area, making sure the liner overlaps the sides of the stream.

❹ Starting from the lower pond and working up the stream, place a large stone vertically up against each step. Pack stiff mortar between the slabs and the lining. Remember that the bottom of each weir needs to be at roughly the same level as the top of the weir below it, to ensure that the water moves correctly.

❺ Position a "header" stone slab over each of the vertical stones for the water to flow over. Make sure the water looks as though it will flow through the middle of the stone before fixing the slab with stiff mortar.

❻ Arrange rocks along the edges of the liner to secure and disguise it. Slowly fill both ponds with water from a hose pipe.

❼ Position the pump in the lower pool and run the power supply cable from a transformer plugged into the electricity supply junction box. Use only waterproof connectors and cables. Camouflage the cable with plants and rocks or bury it, feeding it through a protective conduit first.

❽ Hide with pebbles and plants the plastic water supply pipe that carries water from the pump to the top of the feature. Make sure that it remains accessible for maintenance. Disguise the opening of the supply pipe with a large stone.

❶ **Excavate the stream**

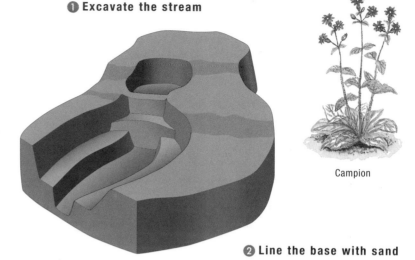

Campion

❷ **Line the base with sand**

❸ **Lay down liner and secure**

❹ **Place stone at foot of each step**

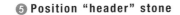
⑤ Position "header" stone

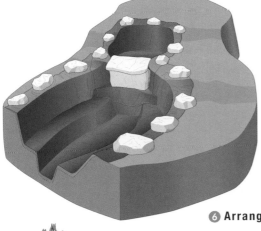

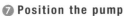
⑥ Arrange rocks around edges

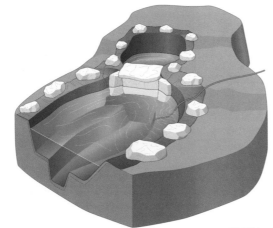

Iris laevigata
'Variegata'

⑦ Position the pump

⑧ Hide the water supply pipe

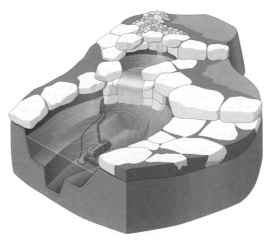

◀ A stream
will need
softening
with plenty of
moisture-loving
plants along
the banks.

POINTS TO REMEMBER

● A stream should start and finish
in a logical manner if it is to look
realistic. If there is no raised ground
to suggest adding weirs, the stream
could emerge from behind a clump
of plants. At the other end, the
water generally flows into a small
pool before it is recycled to the
start again.

● A stream can be quite shallow,
sometimes no more than a few inches
deep. Scatter the liner with gravel or
pebbles to disguise it and create a
more natural effect.

● Allowing your stream to disappear
and reappear out of dense foliage
gives it an air of secrecy and promise,
and it helps to soften its construction.

ADDITIONAL POINTS

● Generally, a stream should be dug out around 1 foot (30 cm) wider than you would expect to need, to allow for crowding plant growth.

● Cram the banks with stream-loving plants like ferns and primulas, for the most natural effect.

● Woodland shrubs, like rhododendron, not only offer protection, but also give the stream a secret, secluded atmosphere.

● If stone steps are not an option, use slabs or rough timber to create suitably homespun stepping stones or create simple bridges for more interesting walks.

The elegant arum lily, Zantedeschia aethiopica, is a waterside flower.

ADVANTAGES

- An opportunity to grow water-loving waterside plants in the minimum of space.
- Excellent for adding perspective to a garden.
- Can be used as a ground-level garden divider.

rill garden

The formal canal or rill is a popular device for creating a visual boundary between different areas of the garden. The rill itself is rarely planted, to maximize the effect of the ribbon of light on water. It is a great way to add perspective to a small garden because it leads the eye in new directions. Here, landscape designer Anthony Paul has used a formal canal to create an unexpected water feature within a much larger scheme; it is partly garden divider, partly a good opportunity to create a bog garden in a relatively narrow space.

On the one side, the cobbled edge of the canal is crowded with lush bog plants to create a wonderful jungle of different leaf shapes, colors, and sizes. In contrast, the opposite bank is restrained by a low stone wall and is home to the kind of riotous tangle of softly colored plants you might expect along a wild stream bank. The effect is simple but dramatic, and achieves a good trick of perspective too, for although the rill is partly concealed by foliage, it successfully leads the eye down the garden and through the dense planting to the view beyond.

▲ ❶ Arum Lily (Zantedeschia aethiopica) is a spectacular waterside plant with dark green leaves, above which rise the huge white lily-like flowers with yellow spadix.

◀ ❷ Japanese flag iris (Iris ensata) rewards the pondside in late spring with beautiful purple and yellow flowers, although named varieties have different color variations.

▶ ❸ Red valerian (Centranthus ruber), with its loose bunches of tiny red flowers in summer, is guaranteed to create an informal country effect.

THE CAST OF CHARACTERS

4 Cobbles
are a good device for edging or for identifying no-go areas in the garden, and are good companions with watery features.

◀ **5** Tibetan primrose (Primula florindae) thrives along pond and stream edges, where it produces clusters of bright yellow flowers.

◀ **6** Purple loosestrife (Lythrum salicaria) is often seen beside natural ponds and streams with its massed spikes of pink flowers in later summer and fall.

▶ **7** Globe flower (Trollius) is a popular streamside plant in spring with its large, shiny yellow flowers and bright green foliage.

▲ **8** Sweet galingale (Cyperus longus) is an ornamental sedge with slender grasslike foliage and umbels of flowers on long stems.

▶ **9** Swan river daisy (Brachycome iberidifolia) has deeply dissected foliage and produces a mass of small, fragrant daisy flowers from summer to early fall.

◀ **10** Japanese maple (Acer palmatum 'Dissectum Atropurpureum') makes an excellent focal point with its bold coloring and ornamental cut foliage.

▶ **11** The flowers of the Scotch thistle (Onopordium acanthium) make a lush and varied display of foliage.

◀ **12** The hardy hart's-tongue fern (Phyllitis scolopendrium) has broad, undivided fronds.

SETTING THE SCENE

PLANTING

A bog or marsh area presents a wonderful opportunity to grow a selection of dramatic moisture-loving plants. Many have unusual or strongly shaped foliage, and even a small bog garden could support at least one of the bolder species for effect. King of the bog must be the Gunnera manicata with its huge leaves and sci-fi flower spike. Rodgersia pinnata "Superba", with its frothy plumes of flowers, is a natural for growing along the banks of streams or canals, as is the majestic ornamental rhubarb Rheum palmatum. The soil needs to be kept moist and well fed to support such a fantastic growth rate.

FORMAL RILL

A straight-edged formal rill can look good combined with a paved area on the patio, or among plants in the garden,

where it makes a strong horizontal feature. Whether lined with concrete or black liner material to give the impression of depth, the edges are usually lined with stone, pavers, or a pattern of brick. Traditionally the rill might open out into small formal pools along its length, or feature simple geyser fountains at regular intervals.

COBBLED EDGE

The cobbled finish along one side of this rill feature combines the well-defined edge of a hard landscaping feature with a more informal feel that is better suited to this location and the surrounding planting than bricks or pavers. Cobbles can be bought in ready-made sets, which makes them much easier to lay and produces a neater, more regular finish.

BEHIND THE SCENES

CREATING A BOG AREA

In order for bog plants to flourish, you need a poorly drained area and a rich soil. Usually this has to be created using a perforated liner to ensure that the area remains sufficiently damp. Often the bog garden will be positioned where it adjoins a pond or stream in order to look more natural, but you can create one anywhere you like, providing you satisfy the necessary requirements.

1 If you have not chosen a natural depression in the ground, dig the area out to a depth of around 14 inches (35 cm). Level the base of the hole.

2 Spread a piece of pond-lining material over the excavated area. This can be either butyl or less expensive PVC liner. Use several large, smooth boulders around the sides to hold the liner in place without tearing it.

3 Repeatedly puncture the base of the liner with a garden fork for drainage, and spread a layer of washed gravel over the lining at the bottom of the excavation to help retain moisture.

4 Insert a length of punctured plastic pipe to enable you to add water quickly in dry weather. Fill the area back up to ground level with a rich, moisture-retaining compost and soak thoroughly so that about 3 inches (7.5 cm) of water remains standing on the surface.

5 Position your bog plants in the damp soil of the bog garden, and firm in well to the same depth as they were in their pots.

▲ A formal rill stretching away into the distance will make a garden seem larger than it really is. Keep foliage back from the water for maximum effect.

1 Excavate the bog area

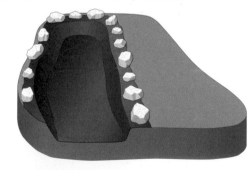

2 Lay and secure the pond liner

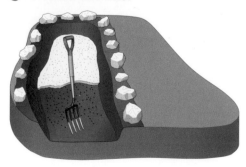

3 Perforate the liner

4 Insert punctured pipe and fill area

5 Dig in the bog plants

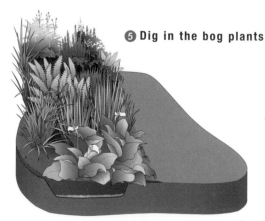

POINTS TO REMEMBER

● You should also provide some kind of overflow facility to cope with excess water in wet seasons, ultimately draining into a nearby ditch or land drain.

● Mulching between bog plants with large pebbles or bark 4 inches (10 cm) deep helps to retain moisture and keeps weeds away until plants can establish themselves.

A pebble or bark mulch will help conserve soil moisture.

CONSTRUCTING A RILL

Rills are perfect for playing illusory games with your garden: a canal positioned across the width of a narrow plot can make it look wider; placed along its length a canal can lead the eye to a spectacular focal point. Set rills in grass to create stunning geometric patterns, use them to define planting areas, or place them beside other features to make beautiful reflections. In smaller gardens, the rule is "keep it simple".

① Use pegs and a line to mark out your proposed rill. Check that your lines are straight and view the whole from all angles.

② Hammer in pegs at 6 foot (1.8 m) intervals and lay pieces of batten on the pegs across the rill. Use a spirit level across and between the battens to make sure everything is even.

③ Dig out to a depth of 9 in (23 cm) remembering to allow for your chosen liner material. Lay 4-inch (10-cm) blocks and backfill with concrete.

④ Check the base for stones or sharp objects, and cover with a 2-inch (5 cm) layer of sand to make the ground level.

⑤ Lay down flexible pond liner and cement concrete blocks onto the base, fixing with mortar between the blocks. Build a wall of bricks, tiles, or paving. Secure with mortar mixed with waterproofing chemical.

⑥ Place a sump in the lower end to circulate the water. Bring the water supply pipe from the other end of the rill back to the pump, disguising it with pebbles and plants—or if the rill is in an open lawn, hide the sump under a grid in the lawn.

Purple loosestrife

POINTS TO REMEMBER

● Rills can be used visually to link other features, such as the patio or pergola, to give a small garden more of a designer look.

● Lush planting along one side of a rill creates a softer effect but still maintains the geometry of its shape.

● Small rills can be lined with concrete. Line the rill first with flexible pond liner, then with soaped timber shuttering. Add concrete to a thickness of at least 1.5 inches (4 cm). When the concrete is dry, slide the timber out to leave the required shape.

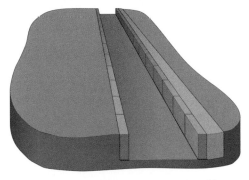
③ Excavate and lay concrete blocks

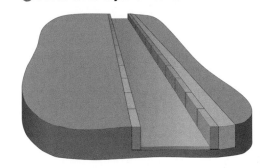
④ Cover with layer of sand

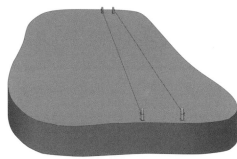
① Mark out your rill

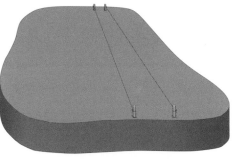
⑤ Build rill with blocks and bricks

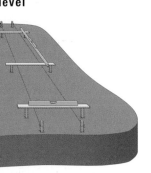
② Check rill is level

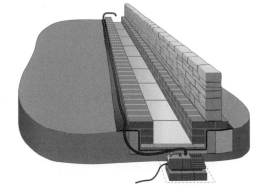
⑥ Complete wall and add pump

ADDITIONAL POINTS

● If you don't have much room for a bog garden, a couple of wooden barrels sunk up to their rims in a graveled area make an excellent mini-feature and the opportunity to grow dramatic bog plants.

● Pools can be linked by a narrow, slightly sloping rill or canal. Ensure that the lower pool, where the pump is located, has a larger surface area than the upper pool, to ensure that it does not empty too much before the system begins flowing.

● In a formal setting, keep maintenance to a minimum by only using a few dramatic plants like bamboo and hostas in containers positioned beside the rill.

● For a garden or patio that can be enjoyed by wheelchair users, raise the water channel to waist height and edge the sides with brick, timber or stone.

▲ ❶ Rocks and stones have to be big and bold to create the right effect, graduating to smaller stones and boulders as in nature. Order more than you think you need and have them delivered as close to the feature as possible.

woodland
stream

ADVANTAGES

● Makes a stunning feature of an existing but unexploited corner of the garden.

● Provides the opportunity to grow some beautiful waterside plants.

● Develops a difficult-to-plant area under trees.

Iris are classic waterside plants available in a wide choice of types and colors.

In this mature country garden, a woodland stream was designed to look as natural as possible within the setting. The stream cascades down from a slight slope built up at the rear in a series of weirs, not only controlling the speed and dispersal of the water, but also allowing a wonderful tiered effect of streamside planting. This layered look is essential to a natural-looking scheme: established trees creating the high canopy, with shrubs filling in below, reducing to smaller plants and finally, ground cover and spreading species in the foreground.

A controlled color palette also helps the feature look as natural as possible; here, familiar streamside species such as elegant flag iris and rock-hugging saxifrage put on a varied show of greens and golds, highlighted only by the occasional splash of red. Although the basic feature is man-made and artificially lined, its style and dimensions are made to look as natural as possible, and its actual structure is concealed by strategically positioned rocks and boulders. A couple of decorative figures have been added as a reminder that this is a private garden, and not natural woodland.

▲ ❷ Sculpture adds a stylish human touch that can transform a piece of landscape into a garden full of interest and surprises. But it does have to be positioned thoughtfully to create the greatest effect.

◀ ❸ Yellow water flag (Iris pseudacorus) is a vigorous native that makes a stunning show of tall yellow blooms in early spring. Keep in check in smaller gardens.

THE CAST OF CHARACTERS

► ④ Ozothamnus rosmarinifolius (Helichrysum rosmarinifolium syn.) is a fairly hardy, erect shrub with needlelike leaves and a silvery appearance. The summer flowers have pinkish buds opening to white.

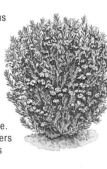

► ⑦ Horsetail (Equisetum) has attractive rushlike foliage to about 10 feet (3 m) tall. The plant is frost-hardy, but needs to be kept in check in gardens or it can be invasive.

▼ ⑨ Ivy (Hedera helix) is an evergreen creeper and climber that is invaluable for filling gaps and smothering vertical elements in the garden. It grows in sun or shade, and there is a variety of leaf types to choose from, including heart-shaped, arrowheads, and many variegated patterns.

► Spotted laurel (Aucuba japonica) is a spreading shrub with soft, glossy leaves and sprays of small reddish flowers in spring, followed by drooping clusters of red berries in early fall.

◄ ⑤ Arum lily (Zantedeschia aethiopica) is an elegant waterside or aquatic plant producing a dramatic white spathe with yellow spadix in late spring.

► ⑧ Saxifraga is a large group of low-growing, flowering plants perfect for softening rocks and boulders. The leaves are usually fleshy or feathery, and rosette-forming, above which a mass of flowers appears from late winter to fall, depending on type.

► ⑩ Escallonia is a shrub with year-round interest, having dark, glossy green foliage and pretty clusters of bell-shaped flowers from early summer right through until fall.

▲ Choisya is a popular evergreen shrub native to Mexico and the southwestern United States, grown for its slender aromatic foliage and clusters of sweet-scented white flowers.

► ⑥ Alpine fleabane (Erigeron alpinus) makes a fine show of pink to reddish purple, daisylike flowers in rocky areas.

SETTING THE SCENE

FLOWING WATER

Part of the appeal of a stream feature is the sense of movement and the mini cascades created by the weirs. In fact, the water is circulated back to the top via a pump in the lower pool to create the effect of running water. This helps keep the water aerated too.

TREES

This garden was lucky enough to have a stand of existing trees to give the feature a sense of permanence and maturity. If you want to reproduce a mini woodland in your own garden and have no established trees, do not be put off. Many species grow surprisingly quickly; alternatively, there are specialist nurseries that can supply large container-grown specimens.

PLANTING

The dense, lush effect of the planting chosen here is perfect for conveying the impression of a shady streamside. There are lots of interesting foliage shapes and shades: from the tall, spiky iris and fat, fleshy hostas to creeping ivies used to fill in the gaps.

ROCKS AND BOULDERS

Rocks and boulders are essential for the natural effect of a feature like this, helping to hide the liner and disguise the sides. Large amounts can be expensive, so to save costs here, concrete has been used at the base and the boulders cemented on top.

BEHIND THE SCENES

CONSTRUCTING A STREAM

The course of a man-made stream needs to follow a sloping site. A pump must be used to recycle the water back to the top of the feature, so gravity is necessary. As well as being a feature in its own right, a stream can link or separate areas of a garden.

Ivy

POINTS TO REMEMBER

● If your stream does need to encompass a change in level, build it as a series of pools and weirs to prevent the water from running to the bottom too quickly.

● If you do add pools and weirs, check the effect they have with a hose before cementing the stones in place.

❶ Mark out the line of your course with pegs and string, and excavate into a series of weirs or cascades.

❷ Firm the soil and level each section with a spade.

❸ Check for sharp stones and position underlay or old carpet. Lay a continuous piece of flexible liner from top to bottom, holding it in position with rocks or boulders.

❹ Build a wall of boulders directly onto the liner at the lip of each weir for the water to cascade over, making sure it is pulled as smooth as it will go. Start with the flatter stones, cementing them onto the liner with a 5:1 concrete mix with proprietary waterproofer. Top with boulders, cementing them in place. Cement between the boulders to prevent the water from seeping through.

❺ To save on stone along the stream edges and help prevent soil from falling into the water, lay a wide lip of concrete onto a 2-inch (5-cm) depth of rubble and slope into the pond edge. Level with a trowel. Cement boulders onto the concrete to disguise it, and soften with plants.

❻ When the concreting has hardened and has been left for three weeks to weather, position the pump in the bottom pool, and fill the stream with water. Use strategically placed rocks and foliage to conceal the pipe that runs up behind to the top header pool, and the electricity cable.

❶ **Mark out and excavate**

❷ **Level each section**

❸ **Position underlay and liner**

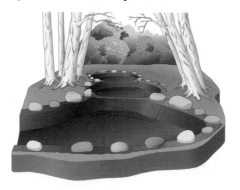

❹ **Build a wall of boulders**

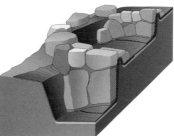

❺ **Lay the concrete lip**

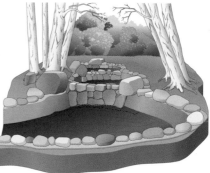

❻ **Position pump and add water**

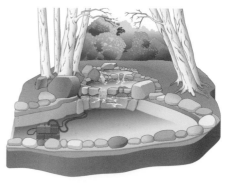

MAKE YOUR OWN BOULDERS

Boulders are expensive—especially large ones—but you can create your own garden rockery or waterfall boulders using concrete and leftover pond lining material or large plastic food sacks. Not only will you be saving on costs, but you will also be conserving natural stone in the wild.

1 Using a spade, dig out a rough hole in the ground to the required size of the boulder. Round off the shape by hand, patting the soil into a round.

2 Line the hole with a piece of plastic—an old compost bag slit down the side or trimming from flexible pond liner would be ideal.

3 Pour in a wet concrete mix of 5:1 that includes cement coloring bought from a garden center, to give it a more authentic look. Leave to harden.

4 When the concrete has hardened, you can pull your "boulder" out of the hole and peel off the plastic. To encourage quick growth of moss and algae, paint the boulder with yogurt containing live cultures.

◀ Large boulders are the perfect choice for edging a stream, but make sure all the strata lines face in the same direction for a natural look.

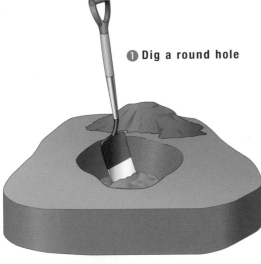

1 Dig a round hole

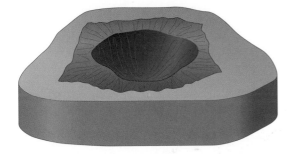

2 Line hole with plastic

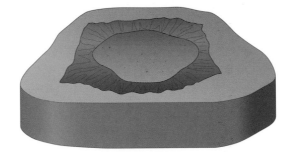

3 Pour in wet concrete

4 When hard, peel off plastic

POINTS TO REMEMBER

● Vary the color and texture of your "boulders" by using proprietary cement colorings and crumpling your liner slightly.

● Man-made boulders are not as heavy as the real thing, so make sure they are firmly cemented in place when building your feature.

● When you have successfully made your own boulders, why not expand your repertoire to garden ornaments too? You can buy the molds through mail order and fill them with concrete in the same way.

ADDITIONAL POINTS

● A meandering, stony course and typical streamside plants can create the right impression, even without water. If time and money makes the installation of a full-scale stream impractical for the time-being, consider a "dry" stream.

● Take advantage of the cool, shady conditions of a woodland stream to grow moist shade-lovers like ferns and primulas.

● For added interest, the lower pool could be developed into a fish pond or terrapin sanctuary.

● Keep invasive plants, like flag iris, in check or they will take over the feature in time. Clumps may be dug up and divided in fall, at the end of the growing season.

large semi-formal pond

▲ ❶ A timber walkway around the pond can be any height—from preformed sections only a few inches off the ground to a custom-made platform several feet high, overhanging the water.

ADVANTAGES

- A bold treatment conceals the limitations of the plot size and location.

- Growing hostas in pots avoids slug and snail damage.

- Being able to walk around the pond extends the scope of the garden.

- Simple construction.

Slugs and snails will devastate the moist, fleshy leaves of the hosta, given a chance. Pot-grown plants can be protected by slug bands.

A dense screen of shrubs and trees, soft drifts of flowers, secluded seating areas, and a leisurely walkway around an extensive pond create a delightfully private place to relax, despite the urban setting. The basic design, by Henk Weijers, is adapted from a strict formal shape determined by the garden boundaries and has been sharply defined by areas of stained timber decking. However, extensive planting has converted the basic framework into a more informal atmosphere.

Greens are predominant, complemented by the occasional soft blue and baby pink flowers, or highlighted by an eye-catching burst of primary red or yellow. The stained wooden bench— strategically placed for observing pond life, or simply for resting— is an anchor point. In contrast, a wicker seat tucked away among towering foliage is an inviting retreat.

The perimeters are boldly planted, disguising the garden's true limits: shrubs, trees, and dramatic bamboo form a background for a dense screen of Ligularia and ferns. The central pond is so lushly planted with marginals—there are even plants in pots along the decking—that its true size and shape is obscured.

▶ ❷ Benches, seats, and garden chairs may serve different purposes, from a secluded place to relax to a dramatic focal point.

◀ ❸ Bog bean (Menyanthes trifoliata) is a creeping waterside plant with pretty foliage and tiny white flowers that spreads well to disguise the margins.

THE CAST OF CHARACTERS

▶ **6** Pickerel weed (Pontederia cordata), with its pointed leaves and bright blue flower spikes, is easy to grow and will bloom from spring to fall.

◀ **9** Crimson glory vine (Vitis coignetiae) is quick-growing and provides good late summer color, followed by clusters of black berries.

◀ **10** Hypericum is a dense, bushy shrub smothered with golden flowers in summer.

▲ **4** Royal fern (Osmunda regalis) is the largest of the species with huge, feathery fronds and good golden coloring in fall.

◀ **7** Flag iris (Iris pseudacorus) makes a dramatic show in shallow water with bright yellow flowers in early spring.

▶ **11** A good filtration system will keep pond water clear and healthy, and will show off aquatic plants to best advantage.

▶ **8** Ligularia dentata 'Desdemona' syn. Senecio clivorum. 'Desdemona' has large orange/yellow flowers, that make a fine display at the pond edge.

▲ **5** Hosta (Hosta fortunei 'Aurea Marginata') makes a dramatic foliage display with its classic broad-pleated leaves edged in yellow.

▶ **12** Water lilies (Nymphaea) are the focal point of the water's surface and are available in a wide range of forms and colors, including double blooms and even one with near-black flowers.

SETTING THE SCENE

PLANTING

Dense background planting is a great device for obscuring the true size and shape of your garden. Trees—even a selection of smaller species—are essential for adding height and a sense of maturity. Build up the layers below with shrubs and herbaceous plants, right down to ground cover for a rich, three-dimensional effect. Keeping the theme predominantly green with only flashes of seasonal color achieves a peaceful yet sophisticated "designer" look.

SEATING

Aim for a variety of all-year seating areas around your water garden; they will provide welcome places to relax and observe the pond and wildlife. Seats could be made of timber, stone, or cast iron; choosing something different for each location can make your water garden more interesting. Position is important too: if it is not tucked away among dramatic foliage to provide a private place for contemplation, then seating can be used as a focal point in its own right, if it is handsome enough.

WALKWAYS

Sound, dry access around the pond will enable you to enjoy the whole garden from many angles, whatever the time of year, and also makes maintenance easier. Dark-stained decking is a stylish choice, but paving, stone, or compacted gravel bounded by timber edging boards would do the task equally well. Narrow, winding pathways may be picturesque, but this more generous geometric design outlines the large pond perfectly and allows room for seating, pots of plants, and a wheelbarrow for easier maintenance.

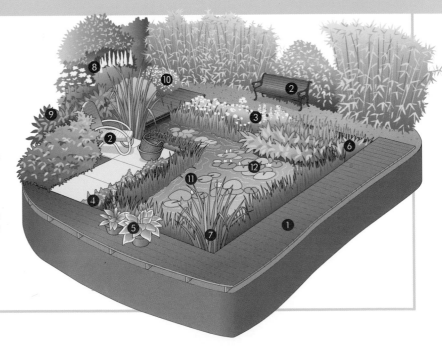

BEHIND THE SCENES

CONSTRUCTING A SUNKEN POND WITH FLEXIBLE LINER

Time spent in accurate construction will be well rewarded by a good-looking pond that requires minimum maintenance. It is important to check your levels at every stage: nothing looks worse than a lopsided pond. Place your spirit level on a plank from bank to bank if necessary, and handle the liner carefully, because a tear means the pond will have to be drained and relined.

❶ Mark out the shape of your pond with string and pegs, viewing it from every angle. Excavate the hole with a spade or digger, angling the sides inward to keep winter ice from putting pressure on the pond sides.

❷ About 2 feet (0.6 m) down from your proposed finished water level, shape shelves 10–12 inches (25–30 cm) wide for your marginal plants, flattening the shelves with a shovel.

❸ Remove any stones or sharp objects from the bottom and the sides of your excavation to avoid damaging the liner. Roll out the pond underlay over the base and sides of the hole, pressing the underlay neatly into all the corners to avoid any bulky areas.

❹ Lay your PVC or butyl liner over the underlay and hold it in place with bricks or smooth, heavy stones around the pond perimeters. Wash it clean before filling.

❺ Fill the pond slowly with water, using a hose. You'll need to adjust the bricks or stones as the weight of the water pushes the liner into shape. You may have to help it fit into curves and corners with some folds and tucks.

❻ Once the pond is full, cut away any excess liner around the edge and use your chosen edging material to hide it completely.

❶ **Mark out and excavate**

❷ **Build the marginal shelves**

❸ **Roll out the underlay**

❹ **Lay the liner and secure it**

❺ **Start filling the pond**

❻ **Fill pond and cut excess liner**

POINTS TO REMEMBER

● When marking out the shape of your pond, try to view it from an upstairs window to get a good overview of its position in relation to other features.

● If possible, rent a mechanical digger for all but the smallest ponds. Renting by the weekend is usually the cheapest option, but make sure you have suitable access to your garden.

● Pond underlay is expensive but you can substitute it with pieces of old carpet if you have access to supplies.

● Measure your excavations carefully before buying your liner, because mistakes can be costly. It is a good idea to put off buying the liner until your pond is fully dug in case you change your mind about its size.

BUILDING A SUBMERGED WATER LILY BED

If water lilies are your passion, you might wish to construct a special bed in the pond to plant them in.

1 After your pond has been lined but before you fill it with water, build walls for a low planting bed about 2 feet x 2 feet (60 cm x 60 cm) directly onto a square of pond underlay on the pond liner. Use engineering bricks or concrete blocks, and a strong mortar mix.

2 Leave it to dry for at least 24 hours, depending on the weather. Then fill the bed with a rich, damp, heavy topsoil.

3 Position a layer of gravel over the soil to help keep it from floating away—and to stop any fish from digging into it.

4 Fill the pond carefully with water as before.

◄ Water lilies need plenty of rich, waterlogged soil to look this good, so consider making a special lily bed under the water.

1 Build walls of beds

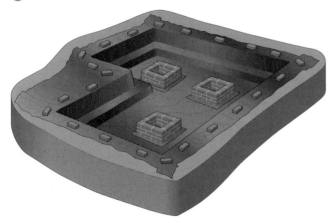

3 Add layer of gravel

2 Leave to dry then fill with soil

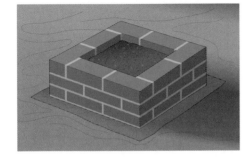

4 Fill pond with water

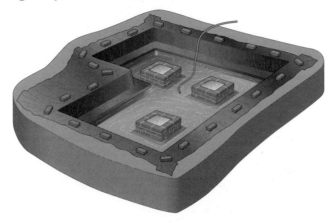

POINTS TO REMEMBER

● The liner will have to be kept taut in the area where you are building. Make sure the excavation is level below the bed, and free of any bumps and hollows.

● Different water lilies require planting at different depths, so check which variety you are planning to grow before you start building the beds. The beds will also have to be at a depth you can wade out to easily, so you can maintain the plants.

● After you use mortar in a pond and then fill it with water, you will need to change the water three times and wait for several weeks before you introduce plants or fish. This is because of the lime content of the mortar. Alternatively, you can use a proprietary pond preparation to neutralize the lime.

a pair of
ponds

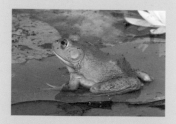

Larger rocks and boulders at the pond edge provide a comfortable perch for visiting wildlife attracted to the water.

Two informal ponds linked by an overlapping decked walkway have been added to this small but seasonally interesting garden. The design gives the illusion of a single, much larger pond, but is far easier to construct. Positioning the ponds at an oblique angle across the plot helps disguise its narrow dimensions. The path is set at the opposite angle, thus creating a snaking line—a classic landscape device for giving the impression of width.

Where space is limited, every corner of the garden has to look good all year round. Here, stone and gravel provide an all-seasons contrast of texture while also serving to hide the pond liner and to create informal but contained borders for an attractive selection of evergreens, shrubs, and small trees. Splashes of seasonal color and important focal points are created by the addition of flowering shrubs, a few carefully selected pond plants, and an underplanting of bulbs, but the main scheme is a restful one of grays, greens, and golds.

▲ ❶ Winter daphne (Daphne odora 'Aureo-marginata') is a pretty evergreen shrub with yellow-edged leaves and purple-marked flowers from late fall to early spring. It is frost-tender.

▶ ❷ Rabbit-ear iris (Iris laevigata) thrives in sun or part-shade providing the soil is kept moist, and will grow in the pond shallows. The yellow blotched purple blooms appear in early summer.

◀ ❸ Yellow flag (Iris pseudacorus) is a robust pond plant that produces bright yellow blooms. The less vigorous cultivar 'Variegata' with striped leaves is better for growing in smaller ponds.

▲ ❹ Winter heather (Erica carnea) is a frost-hardy, low spreading species with densely packed branches, ideal for ground-cover between rocks. The purple-pink flowers appear in winter and early spring.

THE CAST OF CHARACTERS

▲ **5** Many spreading dwarf junipers (Juniperus) make excellent ground-cover. J. communis 'Depressa Aurea' grows no higher than 2 feet (60 cm) and produces a dense mat of bronze-gold foliage.

▶ **6** Japanese sedge (Carex morrowii), a soft, clump-forming evergreen, is ideal for rocky areas beside a pond or waterfall.

◀ **9** Double marsh marigold (Caltha palustris 'Flore Plena') is perfect for a small pond as, unlike other marsh marigolds, it does not set seed.

▼ **7** Juniperus horizontalis 'Emerald Spreader' has long, spreading branches covered in delicate gray-blue needles. It will grow to a spread of 10 feet (3 m) while rarely exceeding 1 foot (30 cm) in height.

▶ **8** Pebbles and stones come in almost endless variations of color, size, and texture. They can be bought by the bag at your local garden center.

▲ **10** Star magnolia (Magnolia stellata) is a compact shrub or small tree with aromatic bark and fragrant star-like blooms in spring.

▶ **11** Dwarf bamboo (Pleioblastus humilis var. pumilis syn. Arundinaria pumila) grows only to a height of 3 feet (90 cm) but produces stems of fresh green leaves up to 6 inches (15 cm) long.

◀ **12** Broom (Cytisus ardoinii) is a deciduous prostrate species that makes a hummock of arching branches with yellow flowers in spring.

◀ **13** Acer palmatum dissectum, like many of the smaller Japanese maples, makes a fine waterside specimen.

SETTING THE SCENE

PLANTING
A strong framework of shrubs and evergreens provides year-round, easy-care interest with contrasting flowers and foliage. Low-growing conifers and junipers make dense blocks of gray, blue, and green below the daintier Japanese maples and pretty Magnolia stellata, and contrast with lusher seasonal plants like narcissi and marsh marigolds.

LANDSCAPING
Washed gravel, pebbles, rocks, and boulders of different sizes soften the edges of the pond, provide wildlife-friendly areas, and help blend with the water. Take time to arrange your material so that it looks natural. Always lay mulch material or matting below to inhibit weed growth.

DECKING
Wood decking can be used to create jetties, bridges, staggered steps or, as here, a zigzag walkway that serves to disguise the edge of the ponds. You can design and build it from scratch yourself or buy interlocking sections complete with fixings and accessories available from garden centers or specialist decking stores.

FISH
A few colorful fish flicking in and out between your water plants offer hours of enjoyable contemplation. Don't overstock the pond: the recommended level is 1 inch (2.5 cm) of fish per square foot of pond surface area.

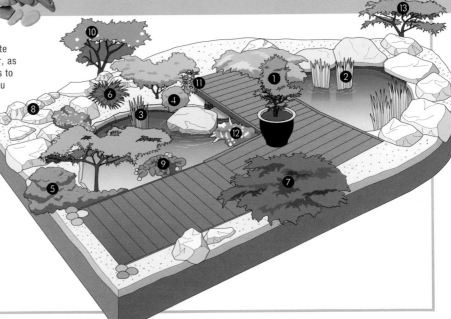

BEHIND THE SCENES

DIGGING AND LINING THE POND

A flexible liner makes an ideal base for informal ponds. Simply buy to size and stretch to the shape you need. They are available in a variety of colors, but most people find that black works best. Liners vary in price, and generally you get what you pay for—cheaper ones will last 5 to 10 years; top-of-the-range materials should come with a 25-year guarantee.

❶ Mark out the desired shape and dig a hole to the required depth, making sure that the slopes have enough of an incline to enable small animals to climb out, but are not so steep that stones roll into the pond.

❷ Cover the base with lining sand to a depth of 2 inches (5 cm) and rake smooth. Use a trowel on the slopes. Line the pond with underlay strips, each overlapping the next by about 4 inches (10 cm).

❸ Carefully position the liner, tucking, folding, and pushing it into place with your bare feet. Large creases should be folded into corners. Bring the edges of the liner beyond the top of the slopes and anchor them with some large stones. Fill the pond half full, allowing the weight of water to stretch the liner fully and smooth any creases.

❹ Tuck the edges of the liner in neatly, concealing them with boulders and vegetation.

❶ Mark out shape and excavate

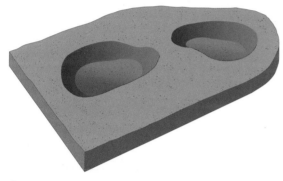

Japanese sedge

❷ Line with sand

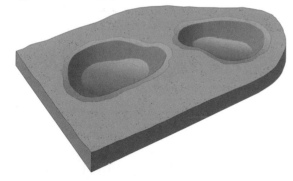

❹ Conceal liner with boulders

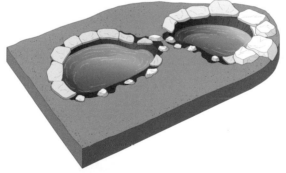

❸ Position lining and half fill pools

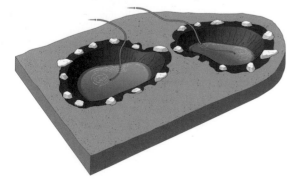

❺ Anchor decking support posts

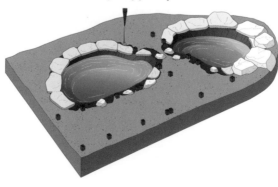

POINTS TO REMEMBER

● Weed-suppressing plastic or membrane should be laid over the area to be decked to prevent plant growth below.

● Wear goggles, mask, and gloves when sawing treated lumber.

● Ensure any hardwood used comes from a reputable and managed plantation source.

● Decking tiles (available at a garden or home improvement store) can be laid directly on the ground to cover a small area. If you plan to overlap a pond or construct a bridge, each tile should be supported on a brick pillar, or on rendered blockwork resting on underlay to protect the liner.

● Special deck boarding is available in a variety of woods and finishes (including non-slip grooves).

INSTALLING THE DECKING

The choice of materials and construction method for your decking will depend on your budget and on the nature of the subsoil to be covered. Pressure-treated softwood is usually guaranteed against rot for 10 years or more. Hardwoods are more expensive, but are naturally durable and look very attractive in a garden setting.

5 Anchor the decking support posts firmly in the ground. Use ground spikes, or bed them in concrete if the ground is very soft. The spacing of the posts depends on the type of wood used; your supplier should be able to advise you.

6 Construct a framework of joists on top of the support posts. Use rust-free fixings such as brass, galvanized, or best of all stainless steel. Screws are better than nails.

7 Screw the boards to the framework, two screws at each end, leaving a gap of around 0.25 inch (0.5 cm) between each board to allow for expansion. Fix a fascia piece to skirt the joists along each side.

8 Continue to fix boards along the framework until the entire structure is covered.

9 Lay rocks and gravel in graduated sizes to form a pebble beach. Fill pond with water.

◄ Blue and golden orfe are hardy and attractive fish, and easy to keep.

6 Construct framework of joists

8 Cover deck area with boards

7 Screw boards to the framework

fascia piece

decking boards

treated softwood joist

support posts on spikes

9 Lay rocks and gravel

POINTS TO REMEMBER

● Always use washed gravel or shingle to prevent pollution of the pond water.

● Larger boulders and rocks make useful pond and stream edgings but can be daunting to maneuver into position. Use a wheelbarrow, or roll the stone along on wooden rollers.

● If you are impatient to disguise your pond edges quickly, try planting pool and stream-side Mimulus luteus. This free-flowering plant grows and spreads pro-lifically in moist soil, or in up to 6 inches (15 cm) of water, producing pretty yellow flowers through-out the summer and rosettes of foliage in the fall.

Mimulus luteus

raised trough pond

There's always great pleasure to be had in creating a thing of beauty from a piece of junk or someone else's castoffs. This stone-effect concrete trough could just as well have been an ancient cattle feeder or a municipal horse trough—perhaps even one of those old enameled kitchen sinks converted to a minipond complete with fish and water lilies for the patio.

The allure of this particular trough is its generous size—large enough to create a substantial feature within the main garden, where its weathered finish, softened by surrounding plants, has a suitably time-honored look. Clumps of variegated reeds cleverly provide vertical interest without obscuring the trough's strong shape and bulk. A large part of the water surface is kept clear, so an intriguing gleam of light draws us to investigate further.

Positioning the trough in a central position, and not against a wall, means it can be enjoyed from all angles. To ensure that it does not look too stark, and to link it with the rest of the flowery garden, it is edged on two sides by large terra-cotta pots of herbs. In winter, the pots can be replaced with tubs of winter-flowering pansies or spring bulbs.

▲ **1** A 'found' pond: a stone trough or concrete feeder makes a great raised pond, but if you are looking for something less permanent that you can take with you when you move, look out for an old tin bathtub or enameled sink.

▶ **2** Terra-cotta pots create a warm Mediterranean effect, especially when positioned in rows or groups and planted with herbs.

▲ **3** Miniature water lily (Nymphaea candida) is a dainty species with pretty white blooms, ideal for miniature ponds requiring only 6–10 in (15–25 cm) of water over the crown.

THE CAST OF CHARACTERS

◀ **4** Variegated bulrush (Scirpus lacustris ssp. tabernaemontani 'Albescens') has all the characteristic features of the classic pond plant, but with the added attraction of variegated foliage.

▲ **6** Variegated sage (Salvia officianalis 'Icterina') is not only pretty and aromatic, but should continue adding interest to pondside pots well into winter.

▲ **English Lavender (Lavandula x intermedia)** includes a wide variety of spice-scented foliage plants with distinctive purple flower spikes.

▲ Sea holly (Eryngium) creates part of the background planting to this feature and is the perfect link between perennial beds and potted herbs, with its strange spiny foliage and thistle-head flowers.

▶ **5** Miniature reed mace (Typha minima) is often mistakenly referred to as miniature bulrush, and is useful for adding height around the edge of smaller water features.

▶ **7** Cotton lavender (Santolina pinnata ssp. neapolitana 'Sulphurea') is perfect for pots, and produces a mass of beautiful pale yellow flowers through the summer.

◀ **8** Spicy-leaved South American perennial Verbena (Verbena bonariensis) with its stems of deep purple flowers from spring to fall, is often grown as an annual.

SETTING THE SCENE

RAISED POND

A "found" raised pond saves a lot of digging, backfilling, and lining and brings the water closer to eye level —an important advantage for wheelchair users. Whereas miniature ponds might be converted from all kinds of household objects—such as old cast-iron bathtubs, sinks, water tanks, and urns—it is essential that the sides of your receptacle are strong enough to take the outward pressure of the water without cracking, and that it is completely waterproof. Don't forget to move it into its final position before filling it with water and plants.

HERBS IN POTS

Most herbs grow well in pots, often achieving a mass of pungent flowers and foliage within a single season. The beauty of growing different varieties

close together is both the natural harmony of their soft colors and the delicious mingling of their spicy scents. The terra-cotta pots are exactly the right height to throw their shock of flowers above the rim, and they do a good job of softening the strong horizontal lines of the trough.

AQUATIC PLANTS

It is well worth tracking down miniature varieties of aquatic plants for smaller water features like these. Tiny water lily Nymphaea x pygmaea, for example, produce blooms only 1- 2 inches (2.5 - 5 cm) across and requires a planting depth of only 6 - 8 inches (15 - 20 cm). The dwarf reedmace, Typha minima, is far less invasive than its big brother the bulrush (Typha latifolia), producing the distinctive dark brown flower spikes on stems of only 3 feet (1 m). Juncus

effusus 'Spiralis,' the corkscrew rush, is popular for smaller ponds, producing unusual curly stems no higher than 1 foot (30 cm). This evergreen plant does not produce leaves, but the unusual stems make an interesting winter display. Clusters of tiny brown flowers appear in summer.

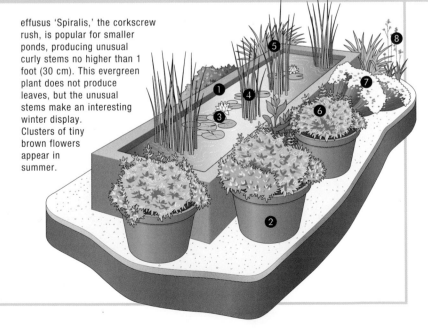

BEHIND THE SCENES

MAKING A TROUGH

You can build a trough in blocks and concrete at a fraction of the cost of buying an original. Make sure you are happy with its position in the garden or on the patio, because you won't be able to move it once it's finished!

① Mark out the shape and size of your trough on the ground and dig out to a depth of around 8 inches (20 cm). Fill with 4 inches (10 cm) of compacted rubble, then level it.

② Cover with a 4 inch (10 cm) layer of 5:1 sand and gravel: cement mix and screed relatively smooth. Leave this base to harden.

③ Build up the shape and size of trough you want onto the base, using blocks or bricks. You will need wall ties to hold it together if it is any deeper than 18 inches. Leave until the cement has hardened.

④ Render the inside of the construction with a 4:1 sand and cement mix to which you have added a proprietary waterproofing solution. It is important to cover the whole of the bottom and sides in one step. Leave it to harden, then repeat the process so that it has two coats.

⑤ Now render the outside, again with a 4:1 mix, and apply two coats, having allowed the first to harden. The finish on the outside of the trough can be quite rough if you are aiming for a rustic look.

POINTS TO REMEMBER

● Never attempt building work if there is any risk of frost or heavy rain.

● The trough should be watertight; if it leaks, sealants are available from aquatic suppliers. Alternatively, the container can be lined with a piece of flexible pond liner.

● A wide range of pigments are available to add to concrete mix to create different effects. There are also tools and stamps for applying to wet concrete if you want a patterned or relief finish.

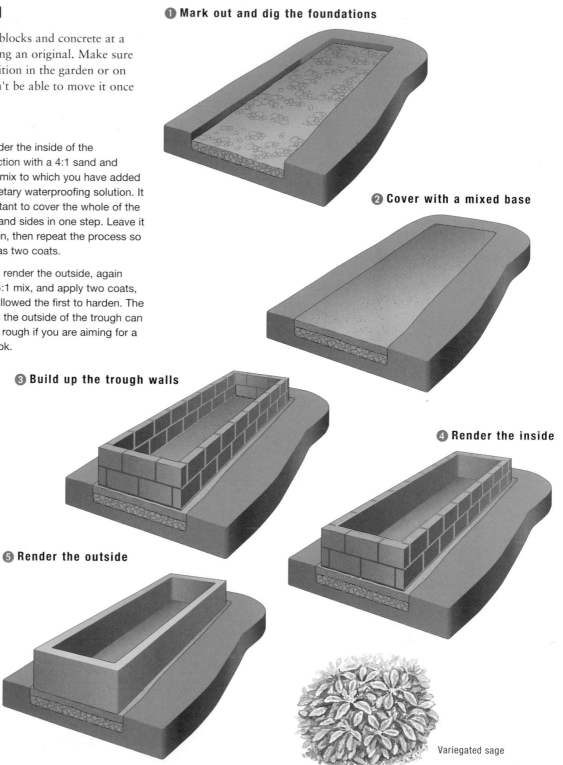

① Mark out and dig the foundations

② Cover with a mixed base

③ Build up the trough walls

④ Render the inside

⑤ Render the outside

Variegated sage

INSTALLING A PUMP

It can be difficult to keep the water clear in smaller water features. However, the addition of a simple low voltage submersible pump is sufficient to run a small filter that will keep the water crystal clear.

1 Place the pump in the trough, fastening it to a plinth on the bottom to keep the pump stable.

2 Join the pump cable to a piece of cable long enough to reach a suitable electrical outlet, using a waterproof connector available from electrical or aquatic suppliers.

3 Run the cable inside a protective plastic conduit and attach it to a suitable electrical outlet. The conduit can be buried in the ground or concealed beneath paving.

▲ Old enameled sinks are finding a new lease of life as garden water features. You can even incorporate the taps!

1 Position the pump

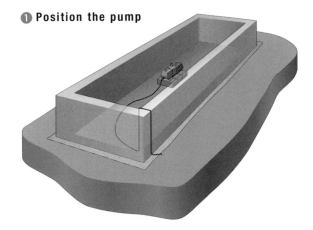

Miniature water lily

2 Join cables with a connector

3 Run the cable to an electrical outlet

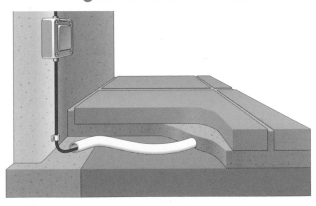

POINTS TO REMEMBER

● Filters can be fitted pre- or post-pump and may be submersible or sited under cover nearby. One of the new combined pumps and filters would be a good option for small features.

● Providing it has sufficient power, one pump can be used to run both a filter and a small fountain or cascade.

● External electrical sockets for the garden should be installed by a qualified electrician as close to your proposed feature as possible.

A combined UV and filter is the perfect solution for smaller water features.

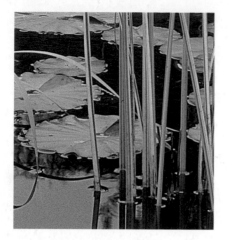

ADDITIONAL POINTS

● For a quick-weathered or more mature look, apply moss chopped into yogurt or cow manure to the outside of the trough.

● Low-voltage pumps that use a transformer to convert electricity from a power source to a low-voltage current are sufficient to run a small filter or fountain up to 4 feet (1.2 m). Larger equipment will need to be connected directly to the power source and should be installed only by a qualified electrician.

● If you are recycling an agricultural or kitchen receptacle for your pond, scrub it with a disinfectant solution and rinse it before using to avoid polluting the water with unwanted fungi or bacteria.

● Keep aquatic plants in check to prevent them from choking up the trough.

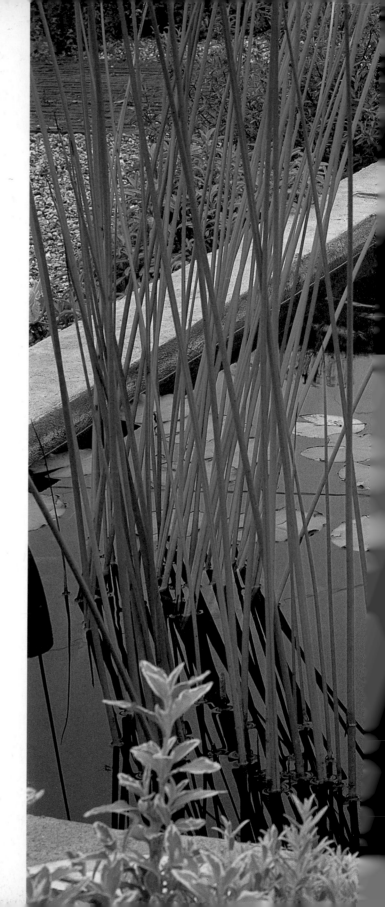

① Mosaic designs can be applied to a wide range of garden surfaces. If a full backdrop seems too ambitious, apply broken pieces of tile or crockery into a bed of concrete on your garden table or glue onto your garden pots.

moroccan courtyard
garden

ADVANTAGES

● Adds warmth and interest, not to mention a more exotic atmosphere, to a small enclosed backyard.

● Suitable garden feature for wheelchair users.

● Easy to maintain.

Flowering cactus create exactly the right exotic feel for this garden.

▲ Garden lighting will extend the use of your garden after dark and can create a spectacular panorama in the evenings. Uplighters beneath large plants create dramatic shadows; string up lanterns or use low-voltage underwater lighting to highlight ponds and water features.

Strong shapes and deep, sultry colors are the defining features of the Moroccan-style Yves St. Laurent garden designed by Madison Cox. Reminiscent of the cooling pools and rills of Spain's Alhambra, the central feature is a tall, central pedestal fountain, from which the courtyard design radiates out into a series of geometric shapes, bounded by the high walls of the courtyard itself.

The raised pond with its striking color and three-dimensional decoration demands instant attention and leads the eye via a formal water channel toward the mosaic back panel, giving this small area a more exaggerated sense of perspective. This jewel-like feature is set in a low-level gravel garden studded with exotic cacti, whose shape and form, rather than color, provide endless fascination. A paved path dictates where to walk, between a series of blue edged planting beds and matching low trellis.

All these structural features, including the rear wall, have been painted a brilliant blue to match the pond. Among such luminous, decorative effects, the planting has to be dramatic and exotic: cacti, bamboo, and a banana plant. Pink paving and soft yellow pots at the corners of the pool offset the massed blue, and add a little warmth.

▲ **②** Ornamental fountains make a great focal point, providing height, decoration, and moving water in the minimum of space. If you haven't room for a pool, there are even ornate freestanding models available, perfect for patios and backyards.

THE CAST OF CHARACTERS

◄ **3** Old man cactus (Cephalocereus senilis), gets its name from the long white hairs that grow from the areoles. Plenty of light will encourage a shaggy look. The hair can be kept clean with a soft brush and warm detergent solution.

► **4** Banana (Musa) creates an instant exotic effect with its large, lush green leaves and yellow flower spikes. This tender evergreen needs full sunlight, away from drafts, and is more usually grown in a conservatory in cooler climates.

▼ **5** Dracaena includes a wide selection of evergreen trees and shrubs grown for their canelike stems and sword-shaped leaves. To grow outdoors, they need warm-temperate to subtropical conditions.

◄ **6** Sansevieria variegata is a variegated form of frost-tender Snake plant, grown for its fleshy leaves and fragrant flowers in late spring.

▼ **7** The organ-pipe cactus (Pachycereus), from the semi-desert regions of the USA and Mexico, makes clusters of tall stems with spines and red flowers.

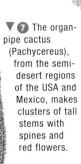

▲ **8** Agave is a dramatic, sword-shaped succulent with tall flowering stems, and is popular in Mediterranean garden schemes.

▼ **9** Tradescantia pallida 'Purple Heart' from eastern Mexico makes a dense clump of purple foliage and small pink flowers in summer.

▲ **Globe thistle** (Echinops) has gray-green, thistlelike foliage and produces striking ball-shaped flower heads on stems.

▲ **10** Echinocactus are distinguished by their prominent ribs and sparse covering of wool, with yellow or pink flowers once established.

▼ **11** Phyllostachys aureosulcata (Yellow-groove bamboo) is very hardy and produces attractive yellow and green striped culms.

◄ **Bunny ears 'Opuntia microdasys'**, makes flat, jointed segments of yellow-bristled foliage.

SETTING THE SCENE

RAISED POND

A raised pond saves any major excavations—useful for gardens with rocky terrain or a high water table, or on a patio that has already been paved. This pool is larger than you usually see in a raised feature and shows how striking it can be if you only have the courage to let it dominate the area.

GIANT PLANTS

Don't be afraid to use large plants in small spaces: they disguise the true size of the area rather than dwarf it. Slightly tender exotics are more likely to survive in the protected microclimate of a sheltered backyard—you don't need many plants to fill it, so you can keep costs down too.

COORDINATED COLORING

In a small area, a unified color scheme can make the space look bigger, even when using a bold shade like this blue. Where your palette of shades is limited, you must rely on shapes and textures for interest.

ENCLOSED AREA

The high walls or trellis of an inner-city backyard can be turned to advantage with a scheme like this one, offering privacy and protection from the worst of the weather.

BEHIND THE SCENES

BUILDING A RAISED POND

A raised pond requires no excavation. It is perfect for a formal patio or backyard where it can be linked to other features such as a rill, raised planting beds, or a second raised pond on a different level, linked by a cascade or fountain.

1 Measure and mark out the area of your proposed pool, using pegs or string, and dig out with a spade to a depth of around 1 foot (30 cm). Add a 6-inch (15-cm) layer of compacted rubble and top up with concrete, leveling with a piece of timber and a trowel to create a firm footing.

2 Build up the wall of the pond with a double skin of brick or blocks, cementing them together with a 4:1 mix of cement and staggering the joins for strength. To build the relief motif along the front of the pool, incorporate a layer of bricks that protrude out from the line of the wall, cutting and filling with part bricks as you go. Fill in any gaps with concrete.

3 For a neat edge around the top of the pond, cement coping stones along the top, or pavers if you want a wider rim as at the rear of the feature

4 When the wall has hardened, render the inside with a 4:1 cement mix, adding a proprietary water-proofer and getting it as smooth as possible using your trowel.

5 Now render the outside of the pool in the same way, with a float or trowel, keeping the corners sharp. Level the top of the rim with a wood strip, pulling it over the concrete. Use a trowel to finish off the edges. When the concrete has dried and hardened, the fountain feature can be installed.

1 Lay the foundation

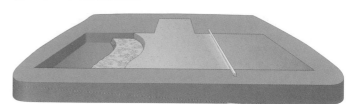

2 Build the pond wall

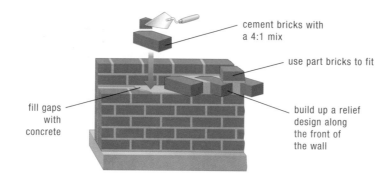

cement bricks with a 4:1 mix

use part bricks to fit

build up a relief design along the front of the wall

fill gaps with concrete

3 Add coping stones to top of wall

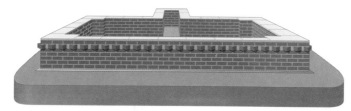

4 Render the inside of the pond

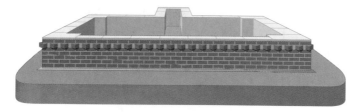

5 Render the outside of the pond

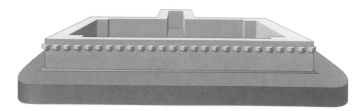

Tradescantia pallida 'Purple Heart'

POINTS TO REMEMBER

● In even a modest raised pool, the water pressure is considerable, so the sides have to be strong. Always make a double-skin construction and reinforce if necessary.

● For a real designer look, choose materials to face your pond that coordinate with other hard land-scaping features in the garden or on the patio whether tiles, slabs, timber, or even mosaic. Paint is another great way to pull features together, especially if you choose a bold or unusual shade.

● The coping along the top of a raised pond can double as seating if you use wide edging slabs or stones.

INSTALLING AN ORNAMENTAL FOUNTAIN

A decorative fountain, whether a tiered bowl feature, a spouting figure, or sculptural work, makes a great centerpiece to a formal pond on the patio, or in the middle of a lawn or drive. Lighting it at night will make it an even more dramatic focal point.

❶ Position the fountain in the pool, checking that it is the right height and centrally placed. You may need to use a plinth or blocks to bring the fountain up to the required height. Cement into position for safety.

❷ Paint the whole structure with waterproof masonry paint—both inside and out.

❸ Connect the fountain to a suitable submersible pump and position the pump at the height recommended by the manufacturers.

❹ Leave for three weeks for the lime in the cement to season, then fill slowly with water, using a hose. Turn on the fountain and adjust the flow, making sure the spray does not reach beyond the limits of the pool, or you will be forever topping it up.

◀ Placing the fountain at the far end of a formal raised pond creates the impression of distance in a relatively small plot and leaves space for lilies to grow.

❶ **Position the fountain**

❷ **Paint the structure**

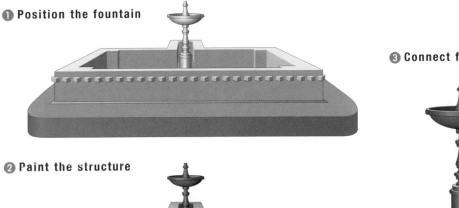

Agave

❸ **Connect fountain to pump**

❹ **Adjust the flow**

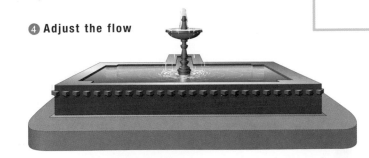

POINTS TO REMEMBER

● It is important to adjust the fountain spray so that it does not overshoot the bowl or pool. Otherwise you will be constantly needing to top up the water level.

● If you choose a windy site, the fountain spray may blow beyond the pool. You can prevent this by sheltering the area with trellis or fencing.

● Fish will love the aerating effect of a fountain, but lilies dislike the disturbance, so grow these in a separate pool.

rocky *waterfall*

The birds and bees will love the slice of wilderness in your backyard.

This large, imposing rocky waterfall has transformed an awkwardly sloping garden plot. Tons of stone have been added in the metamorphosis from mere grassy knoll into rocky outcrop, complete with waterfall, tranquil pool, and lush planting. Cleverly, the rocks have been laid out broadly on either side of the feature to create a natural effect and even incorporate a series of stone steps up to a sunny seating area at the top of the falls.

Although large, this water-dominated garden looks more natural than a steep, narrow waterfall, which so often in other gardens rises up incongruously, like a volcano. To harmonize rather than compete with such a dominant feature, the surrounding planting has been constructed to create soft drifts of shape and color, up the slope of the waterfall and also in the informal beds that surround the patio at the top. The total effect is enhanced by the fact that the garden is enclosed by mature shrubs and trees behind—a suitably green backdrop that does not detract from the dramatic effect of the water feature. The finishing touch is a white painted dovecote with a thatched roof, which leads the eye naturally to the top of the falls.

1 Trees are perfect for adding height and maturity around the perimeters of a garden design and are particularly effective behind a large feature like this, to help it blend in with its surroundings. They are also invaluable for privacy and screening. If you have no existing trees in your garden, get planting now. You will be surprised how quickly they grow, and you can always fill the gaps with trellis until they thicken up.

▶ **2** A dovecote adds instant height and interest to a garden scheme and is easily adapted to both formal and more rustic styles. Here a thatched roof design has been positioned at the top of the rise to give it even more prominence.

▲ **3** Cut-leaved elder (Sambucus racemosa 'Plumosa Aurea') makes a handsome shrub or small tree with deeply divided golden leaves and golden flowers in spring. If you own fish, keep it away from the water, as it is toxic for them.

4 Hosta sieboldiana is a vigorous clump-forming hosta with very attractive heart-shaped leaves and blue gray color.

▲ **5** Acer palmatum 'Dissectum Atropurpureum' is a superb shrub or small tree with reddish purple feathery foliage and stunning fall color.

THE CAST OF CHARACTERS

6 Seating in the garden can be a feature in itself. Often it creates the focal point at the end of a view or in a secluded corner. Here, bright white chairs have been used to catch the eye and attract attention to the top of the falls.

▼ **7** Verbascum chaixii makes striking clumps of yellow flowers on 3 foot (1 m) stems.

▶ **8** Festuca glauca is a clump-forming grass with silver to blue gray spiky foliage.

▲ **9** Allium afflunense is a large summer flowering allium that puts up pompoms of tiny violet flowers on tall stems.

▼ **10** Primula vialii enjoys the cool, moist conditions beside a water feature and produces unusual cones of purple flowers.

▲ **11** Genista lydia makes a mound of arching branches covered in blue green leaves and bright yellow, pealike flowers in early summer.

▼ **12** Gardener's garters (Phalaris arundinacea) is a vigorously spreading plant with large clumps of brightly striped, reedlike foliage.

◀ **13** Iris sibirica is an excellent flower for adding height to damp areas with its beautiful blue, purple, and white flowers held aloft on strong stems.

▼ **14** Iris laevigata 'Snowdrift' is a white variety of this moisture-loving beardless iris.

▲ **15** Polygonum bistorta is a classic waterside plant that looks wonderful planted *en masse* with its tall spikes of tiny pink flowers.

▶ **16** Primula japonica is frost-hardy and clump-forming, putting up candelabrum of bright flowers in the spring.

▲ **17** Flat stones have a rugged natural charm. They can be used for edging a pool, as the lip of a waterfall, or as stepping stones.

▲ **18** Lobelia fulgens, or Scarlet lobelia, is native to southern USA and Mexico, and produces fine tubular red flowers in late summer.

SETTING THE SCENE

WATERFALL
The waterfall shown here is tall but broad, and building it into an existing slope has helped to make it look completely natural. If your garden does not have any changes of level, hummocks and rocky outcrops can be created, often using the excavated soil from the lower pool. However, you will need to landscape the rest of the garden around your new feature if it is not to stick out like a sore thumb.

PLANTING
Suitable plants have been put in *en masse* to create blocks of soft color, to avoid the disjointed and far less natural effect of using lots of different individual plants. Lush waterside plants at the bottom rise up to drifts of cottage-style color around the patio at the top in a subtle blend of pinks and purples.

STEPS
Stone steps not only provide dry access to the patio at the top of the waterfall, but also are an attractive feature in their own right, constructed to echo the look of the waterfall itself. To make walks around the garden more interesting, the steps continue the path across the pool at the foot of the waterfall via stone stepping stones and into the garden beyond.

PATIO
Don't feel obliged to site patios and seating areas close by the house: put them in the sunniest part of the garden. Providing there is suitably dry access, they will be used far more frequently than a chilly spot in the shade. This elevated paved area provides fine views of the garden as well as a delightful sun trap.

BEHIND THE SCENES

BUILDING A ROCKY WATERFALL

A large, rocky waterfall can seem like an ambitious garden project, but providing you get the dimensions right, and take the trouble to construct it safely and authentically, the time spent will be well rewarded with a dramatic and satisfying feature.

1 To build a craggy waterfall into an existing slope, mark the proposed final water level with pegs, and use a spade to dig out and shape the pools.

2 Arrange a length of flexible liner down the waterfall, allowing for the minipools, and hold in place at the sides with smooth stones or boulders.

3 Build up an informal wall of large, flat stones at the sides, overlapping to conceal the edges of the liner, and fix it in place with a spot of 4:1 cement in the center of each stone. The wall can

be built out to create a kind of overhang, which will not only look more natural but will also prevent the water from running back behind.

4 Fill the pools using a hose, and conceal the pipe to the pump behind the boulders up the side. The pump can be concealed under the overhang in the lower pool.

5 Carefully arrange smaller stones in and around the pools to conceal the liner, taking care not to damage it with any sharp edges.

1 Dig out and shape weirs

2 Line pond and secure with stones

3 Build informal stone wall

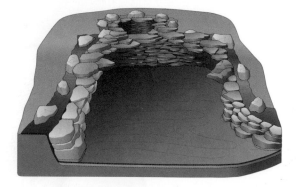

4 Fill pools and conceal pipe

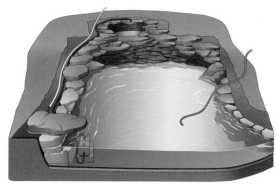

5 Conceal liner with smaller stones

Cut-leaved elder

POINTS TO REMEMBER

● Don't struggle to position heavy boulders unaided. Always get an extra pair of hands or two and use a cart or digger bucket to take the stones to the site.

● If the water tends to trickle down the back of the rocks instead of cascading from the lip, insert a sheet of Perspex at the top to create a falls effect.

◀ Whatever scale it is built to, a rocky waterfall makes a dramatic focal point in the garden.

STEPPING STONES

Any surplus stones can be used to create a series of stepping stones across the bottom pool, providing the water is not too deep. This will have to be completed before the pools are filled.

❶ Begin by cementing a line of flat stones to the liner using 4:1 cement mix with added waterproofer.

❷ Build the wall to about 9 inches (23 cm) high, by cementing on another row of flat stones, overlapping the joins for stability.

❸ Top with a series of large, flat stones, making sure they are the same distance apart and about 24 inches (60 cm) from the center of one stone to the next. Cover the stones with wire netting to make sure they aren't slippery underfoot. Secure the stones to the low wall with cement mortar. Leave the concrete to harden before filling the pools with water.

❶ **Cement line of stones to liner**

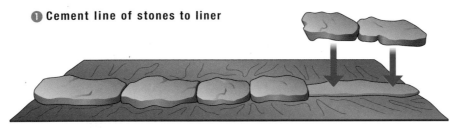

Genista lydia

❷ **Build wall**

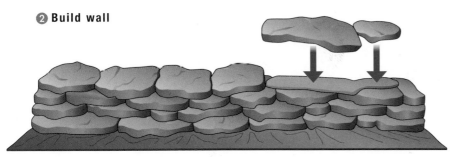

❸ **Top with large flat stones and secure**

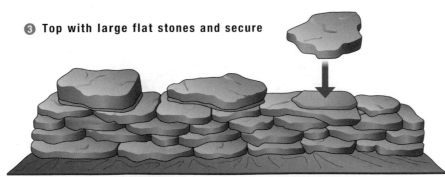

POINTS TO REMEMBER

● It is vital that stepping stones are level and well secured for safety.

● For a more woodland atmosphere across a pool or stream, use thick log slices instead of slabs.

● Growing spiky rushes or reeds in the water beside the steps can soften the effect of larger stepping stone slabs.

● In the absence of a marginal shelf, plants can be positioned in their containers on brick plinths to the correct height.

ADDITIONAL POINTS

● Arrange the boulders so that you can fill pockets of soil between them and plant suitable alpine plants to soften the effect of the stones. This will help your waterfall look less stark and ensure it integrates with the rest of the garden.

● Add seasonal interest with spring bulbs planted among the boulders to show before the main plants.

● Always use a pump which has more capacity than you need, to avoid running at full potential all the time.

● With leisure areas above, as well as below, the feature—as here—it is important that the water garden looks good from all angles. Take the time prior to final construction to get it looking right.

modern decked *pond*

With its bright blue flowers and glossy foliage, pickerel weed makes a bold statement between deck and pond.

This striking modern garden—given over completely to pond and decking—has a rich red and black theme softened by deep green foliage. Designer Henk Weijers has made excellent use of what is only a small space by defying the more conventional use of white paint and pale shades to create the impression of space, and enclosing the area with a high, horizontally lapped fence stained Chinese red.

Far from being imposing, the atmosphere is warm and secluded, the perfect foil for a large, cool, deck-rimmed pool. The basic framework may be formal, but the boundaries of water, plants, seating, sculpture, and walkways are indistinguishable from one another, the areas melting one into the other. There is nothing random about the planting either: although the overall effect is one of leafy abundance, plants are chosen and planted with precision. Softening the fence is a spectacular variegated Miscanthus alongside feathery, spreading bamboo; stands of upright Pontederia (pickerelweed) grow in dense rows alongside the dramatic decking). Even the seating and a sculptural feature marking the edge of the pond are part of the overall plan and treated to a matching stain.

1 Modern wood stains are easy to apply, come in a wide choice of colors, and can transform even existing timber features into something stylish. Finishes vary from natural wood shades to pretty pastels and strong, dramatic colors.

▲ **2** Pondside sculpture: whether a classical figure or the modern pyramid that doubles as a decking rail in this garden, an artistic structure beside a pond makes an excellent focal point and unusual water reflections.

◄ **3** Pickerel weed (Pontederia cordata) is a pond plant that is popular with designers today. Planted *en masse*, it makes a superb fringe of bright blue spikes.

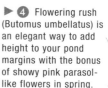

► **4** Flowering rush (Butomus umbellatus) is an elegant way to add height to your pond margins with the bonus of showy pink parasol-like flowers in spring.

THE CAST OF CHARACTERS

► **5** Purple loosestrife (Lythrum virgatum) makes a spectacular show of pink and purple flower spikes along the waterside. It is a vigorous grower, but considered a weed in the wild.

◄ **7** Iris are wonderfully dramatic pondside characters with their large sword-shaped foliage and beautiful butterfly blooms.

9 Poolside walkway: a decked walkway or paved pathway around the pond provides year-round access and many points of interest.

► **12** There are 80 species of bamboo (Phyllostachys), many of which make an excellent focal point in the water garden with their tall, architectural, woody stems and fluttering foliage.

▼ **8** Spiderwort (Tradescantia x andersoniana) makes good ground cover with its low-growing, fleshy foliage dotted with white, pink, or purple flowers.

► **11** Log edging: log piles create a semiformal look and complement decking and other wooden features in the garden.

▲ **10** With its gold and green striped fronds, Eulalia (Miscanthus sinensis 'Zebrinus') is a wonderful ornamental grass for background interest.

▲ **6** Astilbes are pretty perennials that enjoy moist soil beside ponds and streams. They produce feathery foliage and plumes of tiny white, pink, or red flowers.

SETTING THE SCENE

PLANTING

Plants are essential in this garden to soften the structural features. Popular "designer" plants, with their dramatic foliage and occasionally brilliant flowers, have been used singly to create a focal point, or planted in rows or blocks for extra effect. If you want to emulate this design, try limiting your choice to just a few varieties and planting them *en masse*, or keeping to a two- or three-color scheme for plants and features.

BOUNDARIES

Too often, boundary walls and fences are considered little more than a necessity and miss out on any kind of decorative treatment. With so many garden paints and stains available, the options are infinite: from natural timber effects to a weather-beaten bleached finish or strong jewel-like reds, greens, and blues. If the effect is too dominant, soften it with a little vertical planting.

DECKING

The beauty of decking is its flexibility: it can be extended around virtually any shape of formal pond and extended to create fully integrated walkways, seating areas, planting areas, and even sculptural features. Choosing a black stain is a bold move, but here it has a leveling effect on the deep red, and creates a dark, mysterious setting for plants and fish. Another shade, or even a plain timber stain, would have created quite a different look.

POND DESIGN

If space is limited, it pays to think big when it comes to ponds. Giving most of the garden over to light-reflecting water with walkways, bridges, and stepping stones to link different areas can create the impression of space far more effectively than the fragmented effect of lots of little features and a tiny pond.

BEHIND THE SCENES

CONSTRUCTING A FORMAL SQUARE POND

A formal pond makes a fabulous focal point in the garden or on the patio, and can be any size and geometric shape, depending on your building skills. Link the shape to surrounding planting beds, or build a series of ponds in complementary shapes.

❶ Calculate the size of your proposed pond, adding an extra 4 inches (10 cm) in depth and 8 inches (20 cm) in width. Excavate the hole, checking your angles and measurements at every stage.

❷ Create a concrete wall foundation in the hole around the bottom. Soak the base and add a 2 inch (5 cm) layer of rubble. Pour in the wet concrete as smoothly as possible 4 inches (10 cm) deep. Use a tamping block to level it at the top before it begins to spill. Leave it to dry and harden for at least 24 hours.

❸ Using the base as a foundation, build and mortar a wall of two layers of concrete blocks about 18 inches x 9 inches x 4 inches (45 cm x 22 cm x 10 cm). Fill any gaps between the blocks and the soil with concrete mix.

❹ Drape flexible liner over the hole and secure it around the edge with bricks. Pull the creases together and fold them into the corners. Make up a concrete mix of 4 parts clean 0.5 inch (1 cm) chippings, 2 parts sand, and 1 part cement. Spread and level 2 inches (5 cm) of the mix over the base and foundations. Leave for 24 hours.

❺ Drape 1 inch (2.5 cm) chicken wire over the edge of the pool down to the base, ensuring there are no sharp edges. Mortar two layers of house bricks onto the lined concrete block wall on top of the chicken wire, using a spirit level. Support the liner with backfill up behind the house bricks to make sure the water level remains well above the visible liner. Leave to dry for 2 days.

❻ Strengthen the structure by plastering a 0.5-inch (1-cm) layer of fiber-reinforced cement on the inside of the pool. The chicken wire will hold it in place.

❼ After two days, paint the inside of the pool with a waterproof sealant designed to neutralize the lime content of the cement.

POINTS TO REMEMBER

● Do not attempt this style of construction unless you have had experience working with these materials before.

● Never work in wet weather or if there is any risk of frost. Cover your work with a sheet or piece of tarpaulin overnight in any case.

● When making a formal shape, double-check your measurements and angles at every stage to be sure there are no errors, because they will be difficult to disguise later.

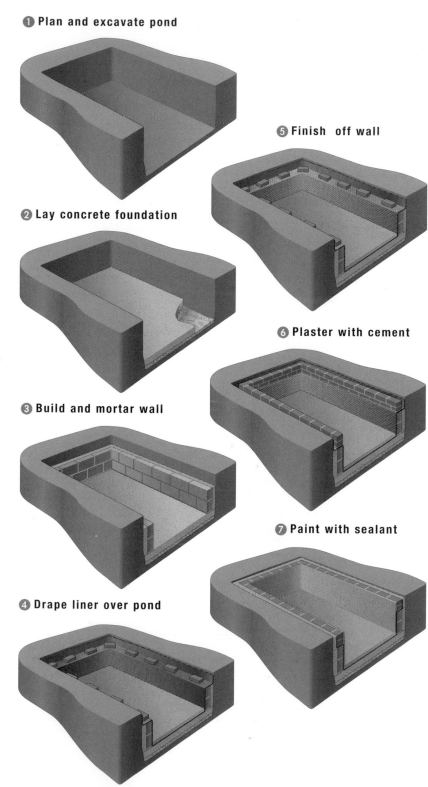

❶ **Plan and excavate pond**

❷ **Lay concrete foundation**

❸ **Build and mortar wall**

❹ **Drape liner over pond**

❺ **Finish off wall**

❻ **Plaster with cement**

❼ **Paint with sealant**

TIMBER EDGING AND DECKED BRIDGE

Timber in the garden has a lovely soft effect in contrast to harder landscaping materials such as stone and paving. Use it as an edging material, or to build decked walkways and bridges to be stained the color of your choice.

1 At 18-inch (0.5 m) intervals, drill into the top of the brickwork. Insert rawl plugs and screw the timber edging into place with brass or galvanized screws.

2 Dig two holes each side of the pond for the 12 inch (30 cm) square joists. They will need to be 4 feet (1.2 m) apart. Fill with 4 inches (10 cm) of rubble topped with a 4-inch (10 cm) layer of concrete.

3 Once the concrete has hardened, steel joist shoes or brackets can be bolted into place using 2-inch (5 cm) wall bolts. Level the timber uprights or bearers. Nail the bearers into place, flat side down.

4 Fix the joists at right angles to the bearers, 18 inches (45 cm) apart with nails at an angle of 45 degrees. You can then nail your bridge timbers into position on top.

Flowering rush

▲ Timbers can be used to enhance the garden in many ways. Here it makes a striking water feature overhead as well as underfoot.

1 Screw down timber edging

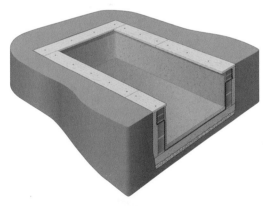

3 Attach timber uprights and bearers

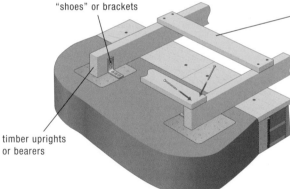

"shoes" or brackets

joists

timber uprights or bearers

2 Create joist foundations

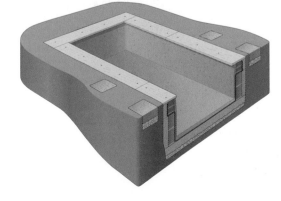

4 Nail bridge timbers into position

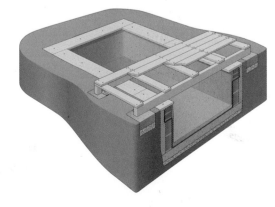

POINTS TO REMEMBER

● When bolting concrete shoes onto cured concrete, predrilling the holes will ease fixing.

● Ask your supplier whether treated timber is safe for use beside or over water. Some treatments can be toxic to fish and plants.

● Decking timber with a reeded surface is preferable for bridges because it is less likely to be slippery in wet weather.

ADDITIONAL POINTS

● This technique for building a formal pond can be adapted to other shapes such as a rectangle, or might be used to create a semi-raised pool where part of the excavations are above ground level.

● Check the timber annually for any damage, and keep it free from slippery algae by using a wire brush or a proprietary cleaner.

● If the garden is to be used by the elderly or unsteady, a stout handrail should be fitted between decking and pond as a safety feature.

● Hard woods are more expensive than soft woods, but they last much longer and require less maintenance.

▲ Select your plants and fish with care, and they will reward you many times over with their beauty, vibrancy, and color.

The Directories

This section features an invaluable plant directory tailored to water gardens, and gives extensive advice on keeping fish and on essential pond maintenance.

plants

Marginals and aquatic plants tend to grow well in the moist, rich soil of a pond, stream, or bog. They are not prone to pests and diseases, so maintenance is minimal, although they can grow prolifically, so cutting back and pruning will be your main tasks. Once grown, bamboos also require little upkeep, but you will need to protect young shoots from rabbits and squirrels.

GROWING BAMBOOS

Bamboos are beautiful and dramatic: just one plant will transform your garden, grown either as a focal point or to create a feathery screen. Most are hardy but may need protection in a cold, exposed site. Members of the grass family, the majority of bamboos will grow to about 3–20 feet (1–6 m) but there are dwarf varieties. The canes come in a variety of colors and markings and most prefer a well-drained sunny site, although there are a few that prefer shady conditions.

▲ Choose your water lily with care, taking into account the style and size of your pond. Some water lilies are prolific growers and may take over.

❶ To propagate bamboos, sever well-rooted sections of the running rhizomes in spring or early summer and plant in well-drained soil or a nursery bed.

❷ Keep sheltered from the wind, and plant out the following summer, having prepared the ground the previous spring by digging in plenty of well-rotted organic matter and a general fertilizer.

❸ Water well during the plant's first summer until it develops a good root system. Apply general fertilizer in spring and summer.

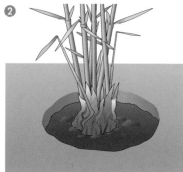

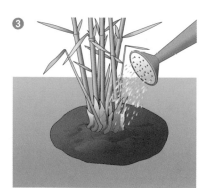

POINTS TO REMEMBER

● Bamboos flower irregularly and the culms that carry the flowers usually die after flowering. To encourage new growth, cut out these culms and feed the plant.

● Established clumps of bamboo need little maintenance. Cut out any old culms in the center of the plant in spring, and cut away any excess growth with a sharp spade if the plant is getting out of hand.

● Bamboos with running rhizomes can be contained by digging a 9 inch (23 cm) ditch all around the plant and cutting off any rhizomes that appear in the ditch.

PLANTING A WATER LILY

Spring is the best time to plant water lilies, because they will have started their growing season, which gives them a chance to get established before they go dormant for winter. A reasonably mature specimen may flower in its first season, although the blooms will probably be paler and smaller than in subsequent years. Take care to choose a variety that suits the size and style of your pond: some varieties are prolific growers and will soon take over.

◀ Water lilies are available in a wide range of sizes and colors.

1 Special baskets are available for planting water lilies, with louvered sides and perforations that do away with the need for burlap liners. If you are using the older, open-meshed type, you will have to line it with burlap or a proprietary liner to prevent the soil from washing out. Fill partway with a proper aquatic potting mixture.

2 Lay the lily plant carefully onto the compost and begin filling up the pot, firming in the plant as you go. It is important that you don't cover the growing point of the lily tuber or rhizome with compost.

3 When sufficient potting compost has been added, top it off with gravel or small stones to prevent any fish from disturbing the plant. This will also help keep the soil in place once the basket is lowered into the water. Remember to keep the crown clear.

4 Lower the basket into the pond and position at the correct depth. Always check with your supplier for the recommended depth, because requirements vary according to type. Bricks may be necessary to bring the basket to the right level.

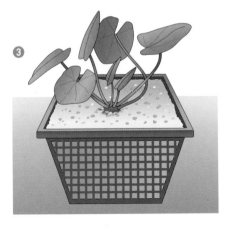

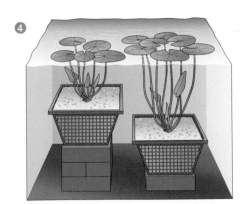

POINTS TO REMEMBER

● It will not be possible to lower young plants to their final depth, because they will be completely submerged. Start them near the surface with about 6–10 inches (15–25 cm) of water over the crown, and lower them as they grow and sufficient leaves develop. As a guideline, there should not be any open leaves below the water level.

● Lilies need plenty of nourishment to flourish and flower, especially once the plants are established. You can add a powdered fertilizer to the compost, but it is easier to use a tablet or sachet that you simply press into the top of the planting basket.

CUTTING BACK MARGINALS

Pond marginals are great plants with their glossy good looks and dramatic foliage shapes, and they grow well too—maybe too well. All too soon that lovely lush effect starts to look out of control and it is time to cut back a little. This is especially important with smaller ponds, where keeping some of the water's surface clear is essential to the garden's design.

❶ You will need to lift the plant from the water to get at the roots—a good reason not to let marginals grow too large and tangled. Lay the plant out gently and tease away any soil and organic matter from the roots.

❷ Trim back excess root growth with a pair of sharp pruning shears. If you want to use some of the root material to grow new plants, cut off pieces of root, making sure each has a shoot, and lay to one side.

❸ Line the pot with burlap to prevent the soil from escaping. Add soil.

❹ Put the trimmed plant back in its pot or on the marginal shelf, replacing the compost and topping it with shingle to prevent fish from trying to nose out the stems.

Water mint

Bog arum

Bog bean

❶

❸

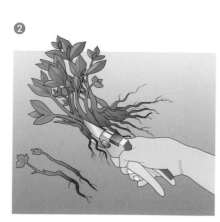
❷

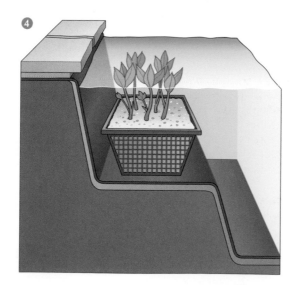
❹

POINTS TO REMEMBER

● Use special marginal pots and containers for your plants: it makes maintenance much easier and prevents plants from growing together into an impenetrable mat.

● Make sure you plant your marginal at the right depth. Some marginals prefer to be planted nearer the surface than the bog bean in the illustration above.

● Most marginal species are rampant growers in summer. Don't let one species become too dominant and swamp the others. Aim for a good variety of leaf color and type, seasonal flowers where appropriate, and different heights and sizes of plant for a well-balanced display.

● Propagating your own plants from root cuttings is a good way to increase your plant stocks; swap with friends and fellow pond owners to increase your range of plants.

● Any root cuttings can be pressed, several at a time, into a pot of aquatic compost and kept submerged in a tank or nursery pond until plants are established.

How to use the plant directory

There is a wide variety of attractive plants suitable for use in a water garden; some will grow with their roots actually submerged in the water, or may be planted in the moist but well-drained soil around the water's edge.

Your local garden center should stock a good range, and will be able to advise you on choice and cultivation. A specialist aquatic center will have an even better selection. When purchasing aquatic plants, remember to make sure that they are nursery grown, not taken from the wild and traded illegally, as this could introduce undesirable pests and diseases to your water feature. Aquatic plants tend to be prolific growers and, at the end of your first season, will already be putting on an impressive display. Be prepared to cut back vigorously at the end of the growing season to maintain good plant health and appearance.

SYMBOLS

The following directory divides the plants into their peak growing seasons, and shows category symbols at the top of each photograph for easy, at-a-glance identification:

Water Lily - this deep-water aquatic grows below the water's surface and produces flat, pad-like leaves that float on the surface. It should not be positioned near moving water and correct depth of planting is important.

Floating Aquatic - these plants float around freely on the surface of the water. They derive their nourishment from the water; some species sink and take the form of a turion or winter bud in the fall.

Marginals—usually grow in the shallows at the edge of a pond or stream. They can cope with standing water or very wet conditions all year round.

Submerged Aquatic - these plants grow completely beneath the water, although they may produce flowers on the surface. They help to keep the water clear and sweet.

Shrub or Tree - plant these for shade and a good backdrop to your water feature, although you will have to make sure that leaves of deciduous varieties don't clog up your pond in fall. Many species enjoy the moist conditions beside water.

Bog Plants - the roots of these plants will not tolerate standing water, especially during the winter, but the plants do require rich, damp soil.

① *Caltha palustris*
(Marsh Marigold) **②**
③ **Height: 9-12in (22.5-30cm)**

This is a plant that will thrive in mud or shallow water. The bright green, kidney-shaped leaves are as attractive as the large, shiny yellow, buttercup-like flowers. There is a double form 'Monstrosa' (UK 'Flore Plena') which produces a mass of foliage; and the white flowering 'Alba'. **④**

The directory shows:

❶ The plant's botanical name in Latin—this is international and is the name usually used in nurseries and garden centers.

❷ The plant's common name—this name is used by most people to refer to the plant.

❸ The plant's approximate height when fully grown, in imperial and metric measurements.

❹ General information—this gives details of the plant's characteristics and cultivation requirements.

Plant directory

The plants in this directory are grouped into seasons and listed alphabetically by their Latin names. The symbols at the top right corner of each illustration describe the type of plant as follows:

KEY

 Water Lily

 Marginal

 Bog

 Floating Aquatic

 Submerged Aquatic

 Shrub or Tree

SPRING / EARLY SUMMER

Spring is one of the best times of year in the water garden. Everything seems to burst into life at the same time. Plant spring-flowering marginals *en masse* along pond-sides and stream banks for a cheering early display, and add plenty of spring bulbs in large random groups for colorful waterside reflections.

Brunnera macrophylla
(Siberian bugloss)
Height: 20in (50cm)

With roughly heart-shaped leaves and sprays of bright blue forget-me-not flowers, this bog plant tends to spread rapidly. There are several variegated varieties, including 'Hadspen Cream'. They are essentially woodland plants, and prefer humus-rich, moist soil with a leafy mulch.

Caltha palustris
(Marsh Marigold)
Height: 9–12in (22.5–30cm)

This is a plant that will thrive in mud or shallow water. The bright green, kidney-shaped leaves are as attractive as the large, shiny yellow, buttercuplike flowers. There is a double form 'Monstrosa' (UK 'Flore Plena') which produces a mass of foliage, and the white flowering 'Alba'.

Anemone nemorosa
(Wood Anemone)
Height: 1.5ft (30–45cm)

A frost-hardy perennial, this anemone produces lots of star-shaped single, white flowers above deeply cut mid-green leaves. Ideally, it likes moist soil and needs to be in the shade, such as beneath some trees along a woodland stream.

Athyrium filix-femina
(Lady Fern)
Height: 2ft (60cm)

A dainty deciduous fern with finely cut, bright green feathery fronds that look at their best when just showing through the soil in early spring. There are several garden varieties with variegated or unusual foliage. They need shade, moisture, and fertile soil.

Cardamine pratensis
(Cuckoo Flower, Lady's Smock)
Height: 12in (30cm)

This dainty plant has pinnate, cresslike leaves and dainty sprays of lilac to white flowers that appear in spring. It makes loose clumps which look best in an informal or woodland setting. It grows well in moist soil, in full or part shade. The double-flowered 'Flore Plena' has better blooms.

Geum rivale
(Water Avens, Indian Chocolate)
Height: 15in (40cm)

The foliage is strawberrylike; the flowers are bell-shaped in pink or cream carried on reddish stalks above the clumps of hairy foliage, followed by fluffy seedheads. This frost-hardy plant prefers a sunny position, in moist, well-drained soil.

Hottonia palustris
(Water Violet, Featherfont)
Height: 24in (60cm)

Floating just below the water, whorls of lilac flowers are held on slender stems above the water's surface in spring. They are useful for oxygenation and fish will also spawn around them. For small water features, the miniature variety *H. inflata* is no more than 8 inches (20cm) tall.

Hydrocharis morsus-ranae
(Frogbit)
Spread: 6ft 6in (2m)

Floating mats, made up of rosettes of small, round, fleshy leaves, produce three-lobed white flowers in spring. The foliage has a bronze tinge and the flowers, with their yellow centers, are rather like miniature waterlilies. It prefers still, shallow water, and may take root in mud, providing useful shelter for creatures.

Iris germanica
(Purple Flag Iris)
Height: 3ft (1m)

A free-flowering damp-loving iris with many hybrid forms. It grows quickly and easily in any temperate climate to form large clumps, each stem producing up to six bearded blooms. The flowers are scented and are available in a variety of red/blue/purple shades.

Lysimachia nummularia
(Creeping Jenny, Moneywort)
Height: 1in (2.5cm)

This creeping plant makes excellent ground cover under bog conditions, and can tolerate occasional light foot traffic. It produces a mat of bright yellow flowers and bright green leaves.

Lysichiton americanus
(Skunk Cabbage, Bog Arum)
Height: 2ft (60cm)

A large, handsome plant with long ribbed leaves up to 4 feet (1.5m) long and striking yellow spathes that have an unpleasant smell. Suited only to cooler climates, they normally grow in deep or boggy ground, and are well-positioned at the edges of ponds. The smaller Japanese *L. camtschatcensis* has white flowers and a sweeter scent.

Menyanthes trifoliata
(Bog Bean)
Height: 1ft (30cm)

This white flowered scrambler is useful for hiding the edges of ponds and pools, producing spikes of pink budded flowers and thick, beanlike leaves. It will spread out over the surface of the water. This frost-hardy plant grows well in mud, and in, or on, the edge of water.

Orontium aquaticum
(Golden Club)
Floater

The flowers are like yellow pokers on thick, white stems, and the dark-green waxy leaves have silver undersides. The leaves may be submerged, floating, or held erect above the surface of the water. The plant is very frost hardy providing the roots are in soil, and will tolerate fairly deep water.

Peltandra virginica
(Arrow Arum)
Height: 2ft (60cm)

Unusual green arumlike flowers are produced above large, glossy arrow-shaped leaves followed by green berries. Variety *P. sagittifolis* (*P. alba*) has white flowers and red berries. These marginal plants work well in shallow water.

Peltiphyllum peltatum
(Umbrella Plant)
Height: 5ft (1.5m)

Mostly grown for its huge umbrellalike leaves, this plant produces pink flowers on long stalks in spring. It will tolerate full sun but grows better in shade. It requires moist soil, and makes a fine marginal water plant.

Primula denticulata
(Drumstick Primula)
Height: 1ft (30cm)

A vigorous grower with distinctive pom-poms of pale lavender to purple flowers. It is very frost-hardy and likes fertile, well-drained soil, part-shade, and ample water. Variety *primula denticulata* subsp. *alba* has white flowers and slightly shorter stems.

Spiraea x Arguta
(Bridal Wreath)
Height: 8ft (2.4m)

This pretty ornamental waterside shrub will grow in boggy conditions. The leaves are ovate with umbels of white flowers all along the branches. It makes a neat rounded shape of arching branches.

Trollius europaeus
(Globe Flower)
Height: 2ft (60cm)

Large globe-shaped blooms supported on leafy stems, they are well suited to the boggy edge of a pond.

Polygonum bistorta
(Snake Weed)
Height: 16in (40cm)

Spikes of pink flowers rise above broad, docklike leaves in spring. 'Superbum' is an improved variety with larger flowers. It will tolerate quite dense shade, but grows in sun if the soil is moist.

Ranunculus aquatilis
(Water Crowfoot)

This plant is a good oxygenator and creates large colonies across the water's surface of kidney-shaped leaves smothered in white, yellow-based flowers in spring. It is well suited to large wildlife ponds, where it can spread and root in a mud bottom.

SUMMER

Make the most of moisture-loving plants' lush, almost exotic-looking foliage and flowers by planning a superb summer display of dramatic shapes and colors.

Acorus calamus 'Variegatus'
(Sweet Flag)
Height: 2–2ft 6in (60–75cm)

The spiky, aromatic foliage and arumlike flowers of this marginal plant will make a good display in shallow water.

Aponogeton distachyos
(Cape Pondweed, Water Hawthorn)

This is an interesting ornamental for garden ponds. Plant in pots of heavy loam and lower into the pond for a spread of vanilla-scented flowers on the surface. The dense foliage may smother waterlilies, if planted too close.

Astilbe
(Astilbe)
Height: 1–4ft (30–120cm)

Clumps of feathery foliage produce branched heads of tapering flowers in shades of pink and white. Various cultivars are available in different colors, from deep red, through pink to white, including 'Amethyst' which has pale purple flowers.

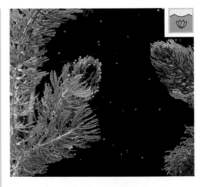

Butomus umbellatus
(Flowering Rush)
Height: 3–4ft (90–120cm)

Narrow rushlike leaves have a purple tinge when young and, in mid-summer, the plants produce pink three-petaled flowers. It likes a warm, sunny spot in the shallow edges of a pool, or in boggy soil.

Ceratophyllum demersum
(Hornwort)

The bristly, dark green leaves of this plant grow in attractive whorls in lengths as long as 30 feet (10m). They do not have roots, as such, but lie suspended in the water. They are considered to be good oxygenators.

Cyperus alternifolius
(Umbrella Grass)
Height: 2ft 6in (30–75ft)

Grasslike spiky umbels are borne on long stems; other varieties offer different colors like the cream-striped version 'Variegatus'. This ornamental species does well at the water's edge or in boggy ground, and is a frost-hardy perennial.

Bacopa Monnieri
(Water Hyssop)
Height: 2ft (60cm)

In shallow water, this dense mat of fleshy leaves produces white flowers which make a luminous carpet-like display during summer months. Keep in check to prevent it taking over the water surface.

Callitriche stagnalis
(Water Starwort)

This excellent oxygenator produces a mat of tiny light green star-shaped foliage, providing good cover for fish hatchlings and food organisms.

Cotula coronopifolia
(Brass Buttons)
Height: 6–12in (15–30cm)

Aromatic toothed leaves and a mass of golden flowers like buttons grow along smooth, creeping stems. The plant grows naturally on mudbanks or in shallow water, but is easily grown in any moist soil or shallow pond.

Elodea crispa/ Lagarosiphon major
(Pondweed)

An excellent oxygenator with dark green whorls of leaves, this plant offers a popular hiding place for fish fry. It requires plenty of light and prefers alkaline conditions.

Fargesia nitida
(Bamboo)
Height: 13ft (4m)

This elegant bamboo grows vigorously to produce many stems of slightly tapered leaves. Dramatic bamboos make superb focal points for damp areas and are essential for Japanese-style water gardens.

Hemerocallis
(Day Lily)
Height: 1–3ft (60–100cm)

The leaves are grasslike and arched;.the glorious trumpet blooms come in shades of yellow, orange, pink, and maroon. The flowers are often scented, and are produced prolifically. They enjoy full sun and moist soil.

Hosta
(Plantain Lily)
Height: 2–3ft (60–90cm)

A superb foliage plant with fleshy, pleated leaves which come in many sizes and colors including blues, greens, and golds, and streaked and striped forms. Leave to form large clumps; hostas are prone to slug and snail damage. Hostas love shade and water.

Iris laevigata
(Rabbit-Ear Iris)
Height: 2–2ft 6in (60–75cm)

Strap-shaped leaves and large blue blooms with golden markings are dramatic for bog gardens and pond shallows. They will thrive in sun or part shade, and can be grown in moist soil, but must not dry out.

Iris pseudacorus
(Yellow Flag)
Height: 2–3ft (60–90cm)

Rich yellow flowers and swordlike leaves make a fine display in shallow water. This is a vigorous growing plant; cultivar 'Variegata' grows less profusely but has attractive striped foliage. It prefers to grow in shallow water, with rich soil.

Juncus effusus 'spiralis'
(Corkscrew Rush)
Height: 1ft (30cm)

Grown for its unusual spiralled stems, this rush variety is popular with flower arrangers as well as pond owners. Remove any straight stems to prevent the plant reverting to type.

Lysimachia punctata
(Loosestrife)
Height: 3ft (1m)

With whorled leaves and bright yellow flowers, this plant can be invasive, so keep it in check. It looks best planted in large groups beside a pond or stream.

Mentha aquatica
(Water Mint)
Height: 3ft (1m)

This creeping, aromatic plant produces lots of lilac flower spikes from late summer to late fall. The short-stalked, oval leaves have attractive serrated edges. They like sunshine and rich soil, and require lots of moisture.

Mimulus luteus
(Musk)
Height: 1ft (30cm)

The yellow flowers are attractively blotched with red, and the smooth ovate leaves are toothed. A good plant for the pond and stream edge, it is frost-hardy and needs part shade and moist soil.

Nymphaea
(Water lily)

Typified by its large floating leaves and waxy exotic blooms, the water lily has an ever-increasing range of colors and forms. Choose carefully, because planting depths and habits vary widely. Some types are too vigorous for small pools. Colors range from white to almost black and there are miniature varieties for smaller water features. If you have an indoor pool or live in a warmer climate, there are some tender night-scented lilies.

Potamogeton
(Pondweed)

A submerged water plant with a preference for the sun, pondweed is grown for its foliage. It is suitable for any pond or slow-moving stream, provided the roots have soil in which to anchor. It is fully hardy and grows best in cold-water pools, but is often prey to waterfowl.

Sagittaria sagittifolia
(Swamp Potato, Arrowhead)
Height: 15–18in (6–45cm)

Grown mostly for its beautiful arrow-shaped leaves, it also produces white flowers, and is more attractive in the form 'Flore Pleno'. It is bottom-rooting and requires a position in full sun.

Myosotis palustris
(Water Forget-me-not)
Height: 9–12in (22.5–30cm)

A mass of oblong, hairy leaves and bright blue flowers with pink or yellow eyes will spread quickly in mud or shallow water to create a carpet of color in the summer months.

Pistia stratiotes
(Water Lettuce)

The pale green rosettes of fan-shaped leaves and trailing feather roots are attractive, but the plant is tender so prefers a warm climate or an indoor pond.

Rodgersia
(Rodgersia)
Height: 2–4ft (60–120cm)

This decorative perennial is as valued for its dramatic pinnate leaves as its white, cream or pink astilbelike flowers. It prefers some shade and the moist conditions of a bog garden or pond edge.

Typha latifolia
(Common Catstail, Reedmace)
Height: 10ft (3m)

Often mistakenly called bulrush because of its thick brown poker heads, this plant can be invasive. The best option is the more controllable *T. minima* which grows to 1–2 feet (30–60cm) and is better for small pools.

Veronica beccabunga
(Brooklime)
Height: 9–12in (22–30cm)

A good plant for pond edges, it produces clusters of bright blue forget-me-not flowers all summer. It is easy to grow in any temperate climate, and is not fussy about soil or position.

Zantedeschia aethiopica
(Calla Lily, Arum Lily)
Height: 3ft (1m)

Waxy white spathes with striking yellow spadices are produced among large, glossy arrowshaped leaves to make this a very elegant specimen plant. It can be grown in water up to 1–12 inches (15–30cm) deep.

Cornus alba
(Dogwood)
Height: 6–10ft (2–3m)

This vigorous shrub makes a multi-stemmed plant with red/purple coloring through winter. Different varieties offer a choice of foliage colors. It thrives in deep ground, and is effective by lakes and streams.

Hamamelis mollis
(Chinese Witch Hazel)
Height: 3–13ft (1–4m)

This particular cultivar of witch hazel flourishes in sun or semi-shade and can tolerate a moist soil. In the fall, its mid-green leaves turn yellow and, in winter, it produces stunning, highly fragrant yellow flowers along its bare branches.

LATE SUMMER / FALL

A surprising number of waterside plants put on a good display of color at the end of the summer season to create stunning reflections. Use a selection of trees and shrubs with dramatic fall foliage and interesting bark or branches to maintain interest through winter.

Acer palmatum
(Japanese Maple)
Height: 13ft (4m)

Modest size, beautiful leaf shape, and spectacular fall color make this the perfect specimen tree and ideal for pondside reflections. More than 600 varieties are available.

Calla palustris
(Bog Arum)
Height: 9in (22.5cm)

The shiny dark-green, heart-shaped leaves are attractive in summer but, by fall, this spreading pondside plant also produces a display of pretty white arumlike flowers resembling miniature 'calla' lilies.

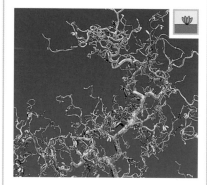

Corylus avellana 'Contorta'
(Corkscrew Hazel)
Height: 10ft (3m)

This slow-growing hazel is prized for its unusually twisted branches, more evident after the leaves have dropped at the end of the year. The bare winter branches are equally popular with flower arrangers. It prefers sun or semi-shade, and fertile, well-drained soil.

Houttuynia cordata
(Houttuynia)
Height: 6–15in (15–37cm)

The blue-green leaves on reddish stems make a colorful display of golden tints in late summer, plus cone-shaped spikes of green and white flowers. This frost-hardy plant likes moist, rich soil, but also grows in shallow water and boggy ground.

Ligularia dentata
(Ligularia)
Height: 2–4ft (90–120cm)

The large shiny green leaves can be up to 12 inches (30cm) across, and the tall stems with orange flowers are a useful splash of color and drama in a bog garden from mid to late summer. Cultivar 'Desdemona' is popular for its bronze-tinted foliage.

Lythrum salicaria
(Purple Loosestrife)
Height: 4ft (120cm)

This dramatic plant looks particularly good in an informal or wild setting, and makes a fine show of reddish-purple spikes in late summer. It prefers damp soil and will spread into the pond shallows. Garden forms can vary from dark red to deep pink.

Miscanthus sacchariflorus
(Amur Silver Grass)
Height: 9ft (2.7m)

This handsome giant grass looks good all year round with its large arching leaves that rustle in the wind. In late summer it produces fluffy panicles of silvery, pale green spikelets. It prefers sun and a moist, but well-drained soil.

Myriophyllum aquaticum
(Parrot's Feather)
Height: 6–8in (15–20cm)

The bright green feathery foliage is popular for trailing over the edges of raised pools, although it can be invasive if not checked by frost at the end of the year. In late summer the tips of the foliage turn red. It prefers sun, but will tolerate part shade.

Osmunda regalis
(Royal Fern)
Height: 6ft (1.8m)

This is a most dramatic fern with huge green fronds that become nutty brown in fall. It tolerates sun, and loves swamps and other boggy areas where it will make a large clump if left undisturbed.

Pontederia cordata
(Pickerel Weed)
Height: 2ft (60cm)

Glossy heart-shaped leaves on tall stems at the water's edge are further enhanced in late summer and fall by spikes of soft blue flowers: a designer's favorite. This frost-hardy plant flourishes in almost any climate, and should be planted in up to 10 inches (25cm) of water.

Sorbaria aitchisonii
(False Spiraea)
Height: 6–8ft (1.75–2.5cm)

This vigorous shrub enjoys being near water and produces large plumes of creamy white flowers in late summer and early fall, followed by berries. It prefers full sun and a moist rich soil in a cooler climate.

Stratiotes aloides
(Water Soldier, Water Aloe)

The spiny rosettes of green serrated leaves look like the top of a pineapple floating just below the water's surface; in late summer it puts up white flowers above the water.

Keeping *fish*

◀ A shoal of brightly colored fish like these comet goldfish add color and movement to a pond.

Frequently, fish are the reason that people build a garden pond; its very size and design will be influenced by the fact that it is to become a vital habitat as well as a garden feature. But fish in the garden are not always afforded pet status: they are just as often considered a living design accessory—that flash of movement and color we expect to see enhancing an expanse of water There is certainly a lot of pleasure in keeping fish— taking time to sit and observe their lazy antics or to experience the thrill of feeding fish by hand can be the biggest bonus of having a pond. Alternatively, your fancy might be taken by a certain breed or type of fish whose shape, color or habit particularly appeals to you, and your fish can become a consuming passion. Fish do require proper attention, but with the right equipment and care, maintenance can be kept to a minimum.

PRACTICAL POINTERS

If you are considering keeping any type of fish in your pond, you must be aware that there are certain requirements and limitations you must satisfy to keep your fish happy and healthy: most ponds can be adapted to their needs.

New ponds are a problem as they do not provide ideal conditions for fish. Before a suitable biological balance has been achieved (as your filter takes time to build up colonies of nitrifying bacteria) any fish introduced may well sicken and die. You must monitor ammonia and nitrite levels daily in the first few weeks after establishing a pond and dilute these toxins with partial water changes. When the ratings seem about right, only introduce fish in ones and twos, building up stocks gradually.

Even an established pond will require partial water changes from time to time to reduce the nitrite level, and to replenish the minerals and trace elements essential to fish health. Replacing around 10 percent of the water every fortnight would be the ideal. You should also keep an eye on the pH level of the water by regular weekly testing—fish need an alkaline level between 7.3 and 8.0. Adjust when necessary.

Another fish essential is plenty of oxygen in the water: a minimum of 8 parts per million, but preferably 15 ppm. Fountains, waterfalls, and filters all help to keep oxygen levels up providing they are run 24 hours a day; but on hot thundery nights, fish may come to the surface gasping. Spraying a hose over the surface may help; or

▶ Pond test kits help to establish the level of ammonia, nitrite, or pH of the water.

invest in an oxygenating bubbler. You should take care to provide some shade, especially with shallower ponds that heat up quickly; ideally around two-thirds of the pond's surface should be covered with water lilies or similar aquatic plant life, or even artificial shading mesh.

STOCKING LEVELS

Most importantly, you mustn't overcrowd your pond with too many fish. The recommended stocking level for a garden pond is 1 inch (2.5 cm) of fish per square foot of surface area. That figure is reduced if the pond is shallow, doesn't have a filter and there aren't many plants. Don't forget

◀ Don't overstock your pond. It will overload the filter and endanger your fish. Aim for 1 inch (2.5 cm) of fish per 24 square inches (48 cm^2) or 10 inches (25 cm) of fish per 100 gallons (455 liters).

▶ A filter can be powered by the same pump that runs your decorative water features.

INTRODUCING FISH TO YOUR POND

Floating the fish in a bag helps equalize water temperature.

• If you have used concrete in the construction of the pond or its surroundings, wait three months before you introduce the fish, or purchase a proprietary concrete sealant to prevent lime leaching into the water. Leave the water for around two weeks for the chlorine to evaporate.

• The best time to buy fish for your pond is in the spring when pond water is warmer. Also, fish will be starting to get lively after their winter dormancy period and will be better equipped to deal with a change to their diet and environment.

• When you get the fish home, float the bag on the surface of the pond to allow the water to equalize in temperature. Don't do this on a hot day, or at least move the bag into the shade. After 1 hour, release the neck of the bag and allow the fish to swim out into their new environment.

• If you are introducing fish to a pond that is already stocked, quarantine the newcomers in a holding tank for a few months until you are sure they are free of disease.

that fish grow bigger and that, if they breed, you will have to reduce their numbers when making your calculations. Equally, good aeration (maybe from a fountain or waterfall) and efficient filtration will mean the pond can support more fish: maybe up to 3 inches (7.6 cm) per square foot.

FILTRATION

In nature, beneficial bacteria break down the toxins excreted by fish into the water, but within the confines of a garden pond, that ecological balance needs a little assistance from a filter, otherwise your fish will become stressed and prone to disease. The basic equipment comprises an exterior box filter powered by an electric pump capable of circulating the total volume of water in the pond every two hours. As well as providing the necessary live bacteria, the filter removes any solid matter that would be otherwise suspended in the water and, if fitted with an UV (ultraviolet) unit, will also prevent the water from turning green. Filters can be disguised behind a convenient boulder or similar pond-side feature.

FEEDING

The efficiency of a pond fish's digestion depends on the temperature of the water, so when and how much you feed your fish is important. Undigested food excreted as waste in cooler weather will overload your filter and lead to disease. The answer is to feed fish through spring and summer with an animal-based protein food, but to switch to wheatgerm-based pellets as temperatures drop, because vegetable protein is easier to digest. When the temperature drops below 50°F (10°C), you should stop feeding altogether until it rises; this may involve taking daily temperature readings.

It is equally important not to feed your fish too much as they will either gorge themselves, or uneaten food in the water will create a pollutant. As a general rule, around 2 percent of their body weight per day is about right. To help you calculate: a 4 in (10 cm) koi or goldfish weighs around 6 oz (170 grams); and a 12 in (30 cm) fish about 26 oz (737 grams). Little and often is a good rule; if this does not fit your personal schedule, invest in an automatic feeder which incorporates an electronic time clock which can be programmed to feed your fish at regular intervals, even while you are away on holiday. Also, it measures out the food exactly, which saves on wastage.

▲ Occasionally, feed your fish live food from the garden as a nutritious treat.

Fish food comes in many prepacked forms, including flakes, sticks, pellets, freeze-dried, and pastes. There are also frozen "live" foods such as bloodworms, daphnia, krill, and shrimp. Many boast growth enhancers, color enhancers, and disease protection. Check the contents carefully, making sure it is suitable for your particular breed and size of fish. Pellets are popular and easy to feed, but do try and ring the changes with a variety of food types. Fresh foods your fish might enjoy include earthworms, woodlice, beetle grubs, and crushed snails from the garden; or wholemeal bread, sweetcorn, and oranges from the kitchen.

◀ Make sure you give your fish the right type of food for the time of year. Switch from animal-based protein food to wheatgerm-based pellets as temperatures drop.

FISH HEALTH

The most common cause of fish illness is poor water quality. This could be caused by overstocking, overfeeding, poor pond maintenance, or—in a new pond—because the necessary filter bacteria have not yet become established. Too-high levels of ammonia or nitrite will spell trouble for your fish, so regular testing of the water before the fish show any signs of distress will head off a lot of problems. Test kits are readily available and easy to use. If they reveal an overload of these pollutants, a complete or partial water change may be necessary.

Too often, problems are introduced to a pond by adding unhealthy new stock. Always buy your fish from a reputable dealer; don't buy fish from a tank where any of the fish look thin, diseased, or lethargic.

▶ Flaked foods are easy to digest and any uneaten food can be conveniently scooped from the surface.

Fish have a natural immune system that will ward off most pathogens (disease-causing organisms); should this be reduced by poor water quality, stress, or overwintering, then ailments can include bacterial, viral, fungal, or parasitic attack. Fish can also be poisoned by pollutants entering the pond from elsewhere in the garden, but more commonly by their own waste products. Look out for symptoms such as redness, ulcers, raised scales or ragged fins; minor bacterial ailments such as these can be treated by improving pond hygiene, regular partial water changes and applying a proprietary bactericide. Sometimes ulcers respond to a cleansing of the wound and to applying treatment (available from a pharmacist or veterinary surgeon) directly to it—the fish will have to be anesthetized first. If the problem persists or looks serious, contact a veterinary surgeon; this will prevent it spreading to all your fish.

Fungal infections often take hold where the fish has a scratch or scrape from bad handling or rubbing on sharp stones; look out for a woolly coating spreading over the fins and body which needs to be treated before it spreads too far. White spot is another common killer of pond fish yet can be cured with a proprietary treatment if spotted and treated early enough. Pond fish may also play host to parasites such as flukes, which cause them to flick irritably or become listless. They are visible to the naked eye and should be treated with an appropriate remedy.

▲ Your goldfish will appreciate a thick mat of pondweed or special spawning mats at spawning time.

HOW TO SPOT AN UNHEALTHY FISH

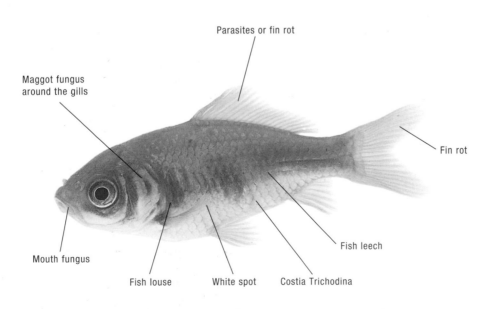

Parasites or fin rot

Maggot fungus around the gills

Mouth fungus

Fish louse

White spot

Costia Trichodina

Fish leech

Fin rot

Most fish diseases are a result of stress from poor pool water, overcrowding or bad handling.

WHAT'S YOUR CHOICE?

Ornamental pond fish have been specially bred to be just that: ornamental. But some are more decorative than others, and the more outrageous types often need extra care, so this should be taken into consideration when making your choice.

Goldfish are attractive and easy to keep with a standard finnage and body shape and any permutation of red, orange, yellow, and white coloring. Elongation of the fins and tail and specific coloring give rise to the "pedigree" goldfish—the Shubunkins and Comets or pretty Sarasa Comet with its distinctive white body and red head. There are goldfish that have been mutated to extreme forms like the Celestial with its bulbous shape and huge wobbly eyes on the top of its head—a curiosity for certain tastes only.

Orfe are another popular pond fish, either in their "gold" or "blue" form, but they do have disadvantages: they can grow quite large—well over 24 in (60 cm) is not uncommon—and they require more oxygen than many other fish types, so it is important not to overstock. Orfe are also extra-sensitive to pond medications, so should be removed to a holding tank before treatment.

The king of the pond fish is the koi, which is specially bred for its size, spectacular colors and markings. Koi are instantly the focal point of a pond, but keeping them is a specialist hobby – see page 134.

▲ Koi need a large pond to show them off to best advantage.

ON THE WILD SIDE

If you are planning a wildlife pond where ornamental fish would look out of place, you may prefer to stock it with native fish species like minnows, bullheads, and three-spined sticklebacks. In this case, provide some movement in your pond, such as a fountain or cascade.

◀ If you want a fish that is relatively easy to keep but a little more ornamental, consider the prettily patterned Shubunkin.

TENDER TOUCHES

Garden ponds in warmer climates would be suitable for the small but pretty Rosy Red Minnow (*Pimephales promelas*) or handsome Shiner (*Notropis lutrensis*), a member of the carp family with silver blue and orange coloring.

▶ Don't mix wild fish with ornamentals. Sticklebacks are very aggressive, with each other; too many in a pond can create problems.

◄ Blue orfe are attractive fish, but do require a higher level of oxydization of the water than other fish.

LESS STRESS

Stress lowers a fish's resistance to disease, so handle them carefully with minimum disturbance, maintain good water quality, and protect them from predators such as cats, dogs, and herons. Densely planted marginals and steep sides will deter most cats and predatory wading birds; if this is not possible, you will have to use electronic scarers or netting. You can buy pond cover nets in a variety of shapes and sizes from your local aquatic stockist; these should be tensioned around 12 in (5 cm) above the water and secured with the pegs supplied, or large stones.

WINTER CARE

Keep filters running in winter but reduce the flow rate during the months you are not feeding your fish. Ultraviolet clarifiers can be turned off. Make sure fish are fit and healthy before the onset of cold weather and hospitalize any with identifiable problems in an indoor tank, so that they can be treated in isolation. Should your pond be at risk of freezing in winter, it is important to keep an area free of ice to avoid a build-up of toxic gases. This might be achieved by use of a small pond heater or, where winters are relatively warmer, a floating polystyrene device. Never attempt to break ice with a hammer or similar blunt instrument as the shock waves may kill your fish.

▲ Protecting your fish from predators by netting the pond avoids stress and fish losses.

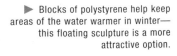

► Blocks of polystyrene help keep areas of the water warmer in winter— this floating sculpture is a more attractive option.

KEEPING KOI

Koi are huge, highly decorative, and hardy colored carp—no wonder they are prized among pond fish. However, they do need specialist care, so check that you know what to expect before you are seduced by a Showa sanke or Kohaku.

POND REQUIREMENTS

Koi are an active fish and they grow large, so although they can be kept in ponds of most sizes, they do need as much space as possible to realize their maximum growth potential: that is, at least a ten-foot swim and a minimum surface area of around 50 sq ft (5 sq m). Koi dislike drastic changes in water temperature, so a depth of around 5-6 ft (1.5-1.8 m) in its deepest part is recommended for better temperature stability. If this seems a bit daunting, consider digging to a depth of 3 ft (90 cm) and building a raised wall of 2 ft (60 cm).

Good filtration is absolutely essential for koi health, and also to keep the water clear enough for you to see and enjoy your fish. There are various types of filters and cleaners available, and it best to consult your supplier before you buy your fish. You will also need a bottom drain to remove solid fish waste periodically. Koi also need shade in hot weather; if this cannot be supplied by surrounding buildings or shrubs and trees, you could construct some kind of pergola structure, a fence, or screen to serve the purpose. This needs to be large enough to shade part of the water's surface and not just the pond edges. Some shade can be supplied by the tougher varieties of water lily, but koi tend to eat aquatic plants, so this will not be wholly successful.

FEEDING

Koi require a balanced, nutritious diet; they are not particularly fussy and will eat a wide range of foods—in fact you should aim for a good variety. As well as specially formulated koi foods, they will enjoy undyed maggots, bloodworms, and daphnia.

▲ Koi soon learn to come to the side for feeding—especially when offered a treat like prawns.

▲ Oxygenating the water 24 hours a day with a fountain or waterfall—particularly in summer—is important in a highly stocked pond.

SOME KOI VARIETIES

Asagi

The Asagi are blue-grey koi with red markings along the sides and belly, and in the fins. They are fully scaled, often shaded like a pine cone.

Shusui

Shusui are also blue fish with red undersides, but unlike the Asagi, they are largely scaleless. They do, however, feature two rows of mirror scales running symmetrically along the length of the fish, on the dorsal margin.

Ogon

The Ogon is a single-colored, metallic koi, usually white, yellow, or golden. It may have white or yellow markings, and sometimes pinecone-type scaling called "matsuba".

Kohaku

Taking their name from the Japanese word for red-and-white, the popular Kohaku should show no other coloring. Ideally there should be a patch of red on the crown of the head, providing it does not extend beyond the eyes or nose. Around the lips is acceptable.

Taisho sanke

The word "sanke" means three colors, and this popular fish is red and black on a white background. The white has to be unmarked and the black very dark. Ideally the fin rays should be marked with black stripes; if the fish has little white and look mostly red and black, it is called Aka Sanke.

Utsurimono

Utsurimono are often confused with Bekko koi, which have black "tortoiseshell" markings on a body of any color. Utsurimono markings are mostly black with white (Shiro Utsuri), yellow (Ki Utsuri), or red (Hi Utsuri), as here.

Tancho

Red only appears on the head of this koi variety, so it is named after the Tancho crane, national bird of Japan, which has similar markings. There are various coloring options including the rare all-white Tancho with red marking on the head.

Maintenance

Providing your water features are well planned and correctly constructed, maintenance can be kept to minimum. The secret of keeping your pond looking good, your plants flourishing, and your fish happy and healthy, is simply to keep up the regular seasonal tasks. That way, most problems can be avoided, and any that do crop up can be spotted and treated in good time.

SPRING

POND CLEANING

A complete pond cleanout is a major undertaking, not just for you, but for your plants, fish, and wildlife too. To give them the best chance of recovery, clean out the pond in springtime, when everything is active, but don't disturb the pond when your fish are spawning. Signs that your pond needs cleaning include poor water quality the previous summer; fish disease, even death; over-rampant plant or algae growth; and a drop in water level indicating liner damage. To minimize disruption, make sure you have everything to hand before you start, and aim to finish the job within a day. Create a temporary pool in the shade from a bucket or paddling pool. Fill it the week before so the chlorine can evaporate and the water can come to the same temperature as your pond.

1 Remove plants while there is water in the pond, and put them on a piece of damp polythene in the shade. Use a ladder or plank across the pond to avoid ripping the liner.

2 Start pumping out the water into a suitable ditch or drain. Remember to keep the pump raised above the sludge level to prevent it from getting blocked.

3 As the water level drops, catch as many fish as you can, Transfer these to your temporary pond with care.

4 Pump out the water to sludge level. Remove the sludge with a bucket or scoop. If your liner is flexible, dilute the sludge with a hose and pump it out. Pour it over a metal grid to allow any wildlife to escape.

▲ The sludge is nutritious, so don't waste it—put it on the garden instead.

5 Wash the liner with a pressure hose, or hose and brush, and pump out the water. Check for and repair any damage. Cracks in concrete can be fixed with a concrete repair kit. If the liner is ripped, either replace it or repair it with a patch. If the liner is old and shows signs of wear, replace it.

6 Refill the pond. Turn on any waterfalls or fountains to aerate the water and dispel any chlorine.

7 While the pond is filling, trim the plants, saving the best pieces for replanted in aquatic compost. Use planting baskets for easier removal and maintenance. Discard unwanted species such as floating pennywort, and replace the plants into the pond.

8 You can put the fish back after a week when the water is the right temperature and has dechlorinated. Do not put back any more than the recommended limit of 2 inches (5 cm) of fish to every square foot.

◀ Running a fountain or similar moving water feature will help aerate the water after refilling.

FISH

As the weather warms up, your fish will become more active. Give them easy-to-digest wheatgerm-based foods to start with, removing uneaten food from the water straight away. Wean them on to pellets; they should be on a high-protein feed by the end of spring. Even if you don't clean the pond, drain off a third of the water and replace it with fresh, dechlorinated water.

REPAIRING FLEXIBLE POND LINER

❶ Before the repair, make sure the liner is completely dry and free from grease or dirt. Cut a butyl or bitumen mastic patch larger than the tear.

❷ Brush the damaged liner with a waterproof latex solution or epoxy resin glue.

❸ Apply your adhesive to the patch, making sure the whole surface is covered. Wait for the recommended time for the glue to become tacky.

❹ Press the patch into position, smoothing out any air pockets.

❺ Paint the area with adhesive and wait for at least six hours for it to dry before refilling the pond.

PAVING

This is the time to spring-clean any paving or slabs around the pool. Sweep up any dead leaves and general debris using a garden vac. Remove spots and stains with a proprietary cleaner and wash down the area with a pressure hose. Take care that any chemicals or dirty water do not get washed into the pond and pollute it.

PLANTS

Tender plants that have been overwintering in the greenhouse can be put back in the pond as soon as the water temperature rises. Cut back any dead material you did not remove last fall, before new growth starts.

WATER QUALITY

Test the water regularly for excess ammonia, nitrite, and pH levels, and adjust it with proprietary treatments. When the water starts to turn green, reconnect your ultraviolet unit and start up any waterfalls or fountains.

▲ Warmer, sunnier days in spring soon turn the water green.

SUMMER

PESTS AND DISEASES

Aquatic and pool-side plants tend to be relatively free of problems. If you can spot and treat plant pests promptly, you can avoid using too many chemicals. Always check the instructions on proprietary treatments to see if they are safe to use near ponds.

Water lilies are prone to aphid and beetle damage—pick them off or hose them into the water where they will make a good snack for your fish.

Slugs and snails attack lush waterside plants, especially hostas. Take a torch with you at night and pick them off or use non-toxic treatments to avoid poisoning both wildlife and the water itself.

▶ Slugs love damp, shady conditions, so specimen foliage plants may need protection.

FISH

Feed regularly, and keep an eye open for fish showing lethargy or signs of disease like ulcers. Remove immediately to a "hospital" pond or tank for treatment.

PREDATORS

Heron can wipe out fish stocks in small garden ponds overnight. If they are a problem in your area, discourage them by netting the pond, or using stakes or wires around the pond perimeter. Herons need to enter the shallows to catch their prey. Other deterrents include flashing lights and noisy alarms.

Local and wild cats can sometimes be a problem. Infrared alarms that release a noisy siren or a squirt of water may help pass on the message that they are not welcome.

◄ Heron are wily birds with a big appetite for fish. Find a deterrent that works for you.

▲ Unshaded ponds are quickly plagued by pondweed in summer. Aquatic plants provide efficient shading—aim to cover two-thirds of the pond's surface.

WATER QUALITY

Sunshine encourages the growth of blanketweed and algae in the water, especially in small, shallow ponds. Shade is a good way to avoid this problem; ideally two-thirds of the water's surface should be covered by lilies and aquatic plants. Alternatively, a pergola structure can be an attractive way to shade part of the pond. Although proprietary treatments are available, blanketweed is best removed by twirling it out on a stick; lay it on the side of the pond for an hour to allow any pond creatures to escape, then put it on the compost heap. Algae can be dispelled by the use of an ultraviolet clarifier which fits onto your pond filter.

PLANTS

In the lush conditions in or around a pond, plants tend to grow rather too well. Remove any dead foliage in early summer and cut back if they grow too rampant. Variegated foliage varieties sometimes revert to green; cut these leaves out to keep the plant true. Avoid any grass cuttings or lawn treatments getting into the water.

DROUGHT

It may be necessary to keep the water level topped up during spells of prolonged dry weather. If you need to top up with a hose, let the water fall from a height as this helps dispel the chlorine. It is important that the liner is not left exposed as it tends to degrade. During times of drought, turn off any fountains or waterfalls to reduce water loss through evaporation. Covering part of the water surface with screens may also help to conserve water.

FALL

PLANTS

To prevent dead material polluting the pond during the winter months, trim back any dead or dying foliage from marginal and aquatic plants. Herbaceous plants should be cut right back to the ground using a sharp knife. Wrap tender species in fleece, tied with twine; if you have Gunnera manicata, cut the stems close to the plant and use the giant leaves to cover the crown.

In colder climates, remove tender aquatics such as water lettuce (Pistia stratiotes) from the pond, and float in tubs of water in a frost-free greenhouse. Other tender plants like Zantedeschia aethiopica should also be removed or put to overwinter 9 inches (23 cm) below the water's surface. Tender marginals such as Cyperus alternifolius and Canna can be overwintered in the house or greenhouse.

WATER QUALITY

Remove sludge from the bottom of the pond using a pond vacuum. A little sludge is essential, but too much makes an ideal breeding ground for disease over winter.

◄ Pond vacuums can be powered by hand or electricity.

FISH

Fish need to be fed well to build up their reserves for winter. Treat them against disease or infection while they are still active. Sickly fish may have to be removed to an indoor tank for the winter. Feed them with quality, high-protein pellets while the water remains above 10°C (50°F). When it drops below this, switch to a wheatgerm-based food, which is quicker and easier to digest. Stop feeding at the onset of colder weather.

NETTING

Leaves from deciduous trees can be a pond pollutant in fall, rotting and releasing toxic gases. Scoop or rake them out before they sink to the bottom, or net your pond and remove any build-up regularly. Netting is available in a variety of sizes and strengths. The finer, stronger types can act as a deterrent to heron too, but it must be tensioned at least 12 in (30 cm) above the water's surface to keep that beak away from your fish. You can buy net, pegs, ties (for joining lengths of net) and frame as a kit, or you can put the components together yourself.

▲ Inexpensive netting will keep polluting leaves and potential predators out of your pond.

BRIDGES AND DECKING

At the end of the summer, replace missing or rusted bolts and screws. Cut out any warped or damaged timbers and replace them. Check that the ironwork has not rusted and examine concrete reinforcing for cracks and damage. Make sure that handrails are still sound. Brush the surface with a wire brush to remove slippery lichen growth and restain if needed.

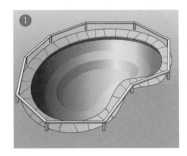

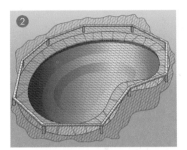

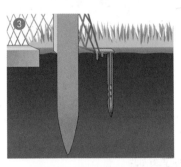

❶ Span the pond with a framework of wooden rails, screwing or nailing the rails together for rigidity.

❷ Drape the netting over the rails for support.

❸ Fasten the netting to the ground around the pond perimeters using serrated pegs.

WINTER

FILTERS AND FEATURES

Keep filters and features running, but reduce the flow rate as your fish will be dormant. Ultraviolet units can be switched off until spring. Oxygenators, venturi, and bubblers should also be turned off as they reduce the temperature of the water. Remove and store them if they could freeze. In really cold weather, fountains and waterfalls will freeze up. Turn off wall-mounted spouts and store the pump in a dry place.

▲ Pouring boiling water into a metal pan will help keep an area of the pond free from ice in winter.

POND

Water shouldn't freeze at the bottom of a pond unless it is very shallow. Large fish will need a depth of about 5 feet (1.75 m). Keep part of the surface ice-free with pond heaters, foil or polystyrene cones—or you can even use kettles of boiling water—to prevent toxic gases from building up. Never break the ice with a hammer as this will scare your fish, and maybe even kill them. Check ammonia, nitrite and pH levels in the water every two weeks.

▶ Give pumps an annual service to keep them running efficiently.

PUMPS

Keep submersible pumps running though the winter, and check for lime build-up and replace faulty seals or impellers annually. When you replace the sump, raise it on blocks to bring it to within 9 to 12 inches (22 to 30 cm) of the surface. Surface pumps should be stripped down, serviced as recommended, oiled, and stored in a shed or garage.

SUPPLIERS

ARIZONA:

Green Thumb Garden Center
1200 Kanis Rd.
Little Rock, AR 72211
Phone: 501-227-5454
Fax: 501-227-5491

CALIFORNIA:

Van Ness Water Gardens
2460 N. Euclid Ave.
Upland, CA 91786
Phone: 909-982-2425
Fax: 909-949-7217

Waterland USA
27071 Cabot Rd., Suite 116
Laguna Hills, CA 92653
Phone: 800-321-6178

Dolphin Outdoors
1808 West Campbell Ave.
Campbell, CA 95008
Phone: 408-379-7600

Lilyponds Water Gardens
(mail-order)
Dept. 1626
P.O. Box 1130
Thermal, CA 92274-1130
Phone: 800-685-7667/
        800-365-5459

Sunset Koi Fish Farm
33920 Travis Ct.
Menifee CA 92584
Phone: 909-508-0722
Fax: 562-860-9310
e-mail:
gschaefer@earthlink.com
www.koifish.com

VJ's Pond Service
10125 El Poquito Ln.
Santee, CA 92071
Phone: 619-596-1905
www.vjspondservice.com

COLORADO:

Spring Time Nursery
23902 County Rd. H
Sugar City, CO 81076
Phone: 719-267-4166,
        719-267-3010
Fax: 719-267-4166
e-mail: info@waterplants.com
e-mail:
victor@waterplants.com

FLORIDA:

Slocum Water Gardens
1101 Cypress Gdn. Blvd.
Winterhaven, FL 33880
Phone: 813-293-7151
Fax: 813-299-1896

*Aquatics & Exotics Water
Garden Nursery*
1896 Walsingham Rd.
Largo, FL 33778
Phone: 727-397-5532
www.aquaexotics.com

Aquatic Eco-Systems
1767 Benbow Ct.
Apopka, FL 32703
Phone: 407-886-3939
Fax: 407-886-6787
e-mail: info@aquaticeco.com

GEORGIA:

Pond Bloomers
5748 Highway 20
Covington, GA 30016
Phone: 770-786-7599
e-mail: Bloomers@mind-
spring.com
www.pondbloomers.com

INDIANA:

Crystal Palace Perennials, Ltd.
P.O. Box 154
St. John, IN 46373
Phone: 219-374-9419
Fax: 219-374-9052
e-mail: info@crystalpala-
ceperennials.com

KENTUCKY:

Reeds 'n Weeds
215 Normandy Ct.
Nicholasville, KY 40356
Phone: 606-887-5721
Fax: 606-887-5775
e-mail: info@reedsnweeds.com
www.waterponds.com

LOUISIANA:

Louisiana Iris
321 W. Main Street, Suite 2D
Lafayette, LA 70501
Phone: 337-232-6096
Fax: 337-233-5673
www.louisianairis.com

MARYLAND:

Lilyponds Water Gardens
(mail-order)
Dept. 1626
P.O. Box 10
Buckeystown, MD 21717-
0010
Phone: 800-723-7667

Maryland Aquatic Nursery
3427 North Furnace Rd.
Jarrettsville, MD 21084
Phone: 410-557-7615
www.marylandaquatic.com

MASSACHUSETTS:

Paradise Water Gardens
56 May St., FN06,
Whitman MA 02382
Phone: 617-447-4711
Fax: 617-447-4591

MICHIGAN:

Grass Roots Nursery
24765 Bell Rd.
New Boston, MI 48164
Phone: 734-753-9200
Fax: 734-654-2405
e-mail: pondinfo@grassroot-
snursery.com
www.grassrootsnursery.com

NEW JERSEY:

*B&M Aquatic Garden
& Koi Center*
Route 94,
Hamburg, NJ, 07419
Phone: 201-209-1185
Fax: 201-827-4232

Waterford Gardens
74 East Allendale Rd., Dept. F
Saddle River, NJ 07458
Phone: 201-327-0721

NEW YORK:

Scherer Water Gardens
104 Waterside Rd.
Northport, NY 11768
Phone: 516-261-7432
Fax: 516-261-9325

Hermitage Garden Pools
(mail-order)
P.O. Box 361, Dept. A
Castanoga, NY 13032
Phone: 315-697-9093

NORTH CAROLINA:

Perry's Water Gardens
191 Leatherman Gap Rd.
Franklin, NC 28734
Phone: 704-524-3264
Fax: 704-369-2050

OHIO:

William Tricker, Inc.
7125 Tanglewood Dr.
Independence, OH 44131
Phone: 216-524-3491

OKLAHOMA:

Water's Edge Aquatic Nursery
2775 Hardin Rd.
Choctaw OK 73020
Phone: 405-737-0003
e-mail:
fred@watersedgenursery.com
www.watersedgenursery.com

OREGON:

Hughes Water Gardens
25289 SW Stafford Rd.
Tualatin, OR 97062
Phone: 503-638-1709/
          800-858-1709
Fax: 503-638-9035
e-mail: water@teleport.com

TENNESSEE:

The Water Garden
5594 Dayton Blvd.
Chattanooga TN 37415
Phone: 423-870-2838
Fax: 423-870-3382
e-mail: info@watergarden.com
www.thewatergarden.com

TEXAS:

Lilyponds Water Gardens
(mail-order)
Dept. 1626
P.O. Box 188
Brookshire, TX 77423-0188
Phone: 800-766-5648

INDEX

CREDITS

Quarto would like to thank and acknowledge the following for supplying pictures reproduced in this book:

Key: B = Bottom, T = Top, C = Center, L = Left, R = Right

Bradshaw's Direct 19C & CR, 51BL, 93BR, 96TR, 138B.
Clive Nichols Garden Pictures 22–23 (J Williams. H Peschar Gallery), 42T, 44TL & 46–47 (Mr. Fraser/J Treyer-Evans), 84T, 86TL & 88–89 (designer: Richard Coward), 96T, 98TL & 100–101 (Designer: Madison Cox). **CMS Gardens** (further details at www.cmsgardens.co.uk) 14TC, TR & CR, 16L & C, 17BL & BC, 19B, 45TR, 63TR, 81TR, 129BC. **Dave Bevan** 17R, 19TR, 21BR, 30R, 49TL, 50TR, 61C & R, 72CR, 75TR, 78TR, 87TR, 93TR, 108TR, 109CR, 116TR, 120BL & BC, 121TL, TCL, TC, TR & BC, 122TL, BL, BCL & TC, 123BCL, TC, TR & BR, 124TL, BCL & TC, 125BL & TR, 127BCL & BC, 128L, 129TR, 130BR, 131TR & BR, 132TL, BL & BR, 133TL & BL, 134–135 (all images), 136BL & R, 137TR & BR, 138L, 139L. **Eric Sawford** 12TR, 120BCL & TC, 126TC, 127TC. **Garden Picture Library** 30T, 32TL & 34–35 (Eric Crichton), 36T, 38TL & 40–41 (Christi Carter), 48T, 50TL & 52–53 (J S Sira), 54T, 56TL & 58–59 (Marie O'Hara), 60T, 62TL & 64–65 (Brigitte Thomas), 66T, 68TL & 70–71 (Ron Sutherland), 78T, 80TL & 82–83 (Steven Wooster), 90T, 92TL & 94–95 (Michael Paul), 108T, 110TL & 112–113 (Steven Wooster). **Harry Smith Collection** 7, 8TL, 10–11, 20CR, 24T, 26TL & 28–29, 102T, 104TL & 106–10, 111TR, 120BR, 121BR, 123BL & BC, 125TC, 127TCL, 133BR. **Heather Angel** 78BL, 129CL, 130L. **Jerry Pavia** 19CL, 72T, 74TL & 76–77, 114–115. **Oasis Water Garden Products UK** (www.oasis–water–gardens.com) 14C, 17T, 19R, 129BL, 130TC. **Peter May** 2–3, 13BL, 139BL & BR. **Peter Stiles** 6TC, 20TL, 68TR. **World of Water** (photography: Jessica Husband) 9B, 18TR, 33TR, 36TR, 39TR, 42R, 54R & BR, 56TR, 96BR, 99TR, 105TL.

All other photographs and illustrations are the copyright of Quarto. While every effort has been made to credit contributors, we apologize in advance if there have been any omissions or errors.